Narcissus Transformed

Literature & Philosophy

A. J. Cascardi, General Editor

This new series will publish books in a wide range of subjects in philosophy and literature, including studies of the social and historical issues that relate these two fields. Drawing on the resources of the Anglo-American and Continental traditions, the series will be open to philosophically informed scholarship covering the entire range of contemporary critical thought.

Already published:

J. M. Bernstein, *The Fate of Art: Aesthetic Alienation from Kant to Derrida and Adorno*

Mary E. Finn, *Writing the Incommensurable: Kierkegaard, Rossetti, and Hopkins*

Robert Steiner, *Toward a Grammar of Abstraction: Modernity, Wittgenstein, and the Paintings of Jackson Pollock*

Reed Way Dasenbrock, ed., *Literary Theory After Davidson*

Peter Bürger, *The Decline of Modernism*

David Jacobson, *Emerson's Pragmatic Vision: The Dance of the Eye*

Narcissus Transformed

THE TEXTUAL SUBJECT
in PSYCHOANALYSIS *and* LITERATURE

Gray Kochhar-Lindgren

The Pennsylvania State University Press
University Park, Pennsylvania

Library of Congress Cataloging-in-Publication Data

Kochhar-Lindgren, Gray.
    Narcissus transformed : the textual subject in psychoanalysis and
literature / Gray Kochhar-Lindgren.
        p.   cm.
    Includes bibliographical references and index.
    ISBN 0-271-00907-1 (alk. paper)
    1. English fiction—20th century—History and criticism—Theory,
etc.   2. Narcissus (Greek mythology) in literature.   3. Fowles,
John, 1926– Daniel Martin.   4. Woolf, Virginia, 1882–1941. Waves.
5. Tournier, Michel. Roi des Aulnes.   6. Psychoanalysis and
literature.   7. Narcissism in literature.   8. Self in literature.
I. Title.
PR888.N355K63   1993
823'.9109353—dc20   92-30296
                                                              CIP

Published by The Pennsylvania State University Press,
Suite C, Barbara Building, University Park, PA 16802-1003

It is the policy of The Pennsylvania State University Press to use acid-free paper for
the first printing of all clothbound books. Publications on uncoated stock satisfy the
minimum requirements of American National Standard for Information Sciences—
Permanence of Paper for Printed Library Materials, ANSI Z39.48–1984.

Contents

Acknowledgments

Writing calls forth readings, and this book has had the good fortune to pass through the hands of a number of accomplished readers. Robert Detweiler has been unwaveringly encouraging about the project from its inception; Robert Paul showed me a number of paths into the worlds of psychoanalysis; Walter Reed has consistently supported my interdisciplinary approach to literature; and William Doty has reminded me about the complex world of myth. Anthony J. Cascardi and Juliet Flower Mac-Cannell offered astute criticisms of the work that led to significant revisions of earlier drafts. Philip Winsor, senior editor at Penn State, guided the book through the convolutions of the editorial decision-making process. I am grateful to each of these people for the intelligence of their comments and for their support of the book. I am grateful, as well, to David Price and Keith Belton for their insatiable reading habits.

Very special thanks of a different sort go to Duncan, for making sure that I know something about industrial lumberjacking, chess, and the imagination. Finally, I owe the deepest debt of gratitude to Kanta, who teaches me about both the multiplicity of vision and the singleness of purpose. This book is dedicated to her.

1

The Obsessive Gaze:
The Logic of Narcissism in
Contemporary Discourse

He looks in wonder,
Charmed by himself, spell-bound, and no more moving
Than any marble statue.

—Ovid, *Metamorphoses*

The figure of Narcissus haunts the twentieth century. A beautiful young man who gazes neither at the world around him nor at those who reach for him with desire, Narcissus longs only for the possession of the evanescent reflection of himself that shimmers in a glassy pond. This obsessive self-reflection leads not to the wisdom of self-understanding, which reflection so often claims for itself, but to death: Narcissus's own and that of Echo, the primary other of the tale. The narcissistic logic of this self-reflection, which is simultaneously murderous and suicidal, is a truncated symbolic dialectic that lacks the capacity to recognize that which is other than itself.

In the following investigation, I examine the narcissistic dialectic with two main ends in view: to explore the entextualization of the human subject as it occurs in psychoanalysis and in fiction—modes of discourse that are intimately related—and to determine the beginnings of a way "beyond narcissism" that is enacted through a dialectic of fictionalizing that breaks the entombing, rigidifying gaze of the selfsame that is so dear to the heart of Narcissus and to Western culture. Throughout the process, I am interested in the relationships among art, the textual subject, and death.

This reflection on a certain type of self-reflection occurs on the borders of the narcissistic mythos, a field of figural signification that includes not only the characters from Ovid's rendition of the narrative in *Metamorphoses*—Narcissus's parents Liriope and Cephisus, Tiresias, Echo, the spurned lovers of Narcissus, and Nemesis, who answers the prayer for his destruction—but also the more encompassing discourses of philosophy, psychoanalysis, and literature. A narrative that spans discourses in such a way is a myth, a narrative paradigm that creative interpretation rejuvenates at various cultural moments for various cultural reasons.

Narcissus, a rather minor character metamorphosed by Ovid—he becomes the flower that lures Persephone to her meeting with Hades—has *become* mythic in stature by the historical accretion of meanings and by the fact that the narrative continues to do mythic work in postmodern culture. Before I add my own piece of work through a detailed reading of narcissism and the textual subject in Sigmund Freud, Jacques Lacan, and three modern novelists—Virginia Woolf, Michel Tournier, and John Fowles—I examine first the Cartesian foundation of philosophical narcissism, the centrality of Narcissus to fiction, and the necessity of the ruse of metaphor and the "mythicity" of myth in any "transformation" of narcissism.

To enter the narrative hall of mirrors that Narcissus produces is to become immediately spellbound by an enchantment that will unavoidably entail a prolonged interaction with illusion and the tricks of metaphor, myth, and fiction. The risk of looking at the subject and textuality, art and death, through the mirror of Narcissus is that this looking-glass will inevitably distort all the objects it reflects. We will not be able to trust the form or direction of our own arguments; we will founder on the knowledge that by engaging in a prolonged reflection on narcissism, we also recapitulate the rigidifying logic of narcissism.

But writing entails risks, and more important, it is just the odd particularity of vision engendered by the choice of this poetic narrative that will itself provide the material for thinking about the place of the fictive—the short-lived but recurring reflections in the water—in the discussion of literature, psychoanalysis, and the enigma of the human subjectivity. And an "enigma" (derived from the Greek *ainos,* a story) is a "rhetorical form" like a "riddle, parable, [or] a prophetic vision" (D. Miller, 390). It is a mode of seeing darkly, and to see darkly (like the Sphinx, Tiresias, or Heraclitus, for instance) is to see with different eyes than those who—like Oedipus, Narcissus, and Descartes—desire above all things the "clear and distinct."

But if the myth of Narcissus will shape our understanding of literature, psychoanalysis, and philosophies of reflection, these, in their turn, have already in part determined our appropriation of Narcissus, a figure who already "belongs" to the traditions of Descartes, Freud, and the novel (and before these, to theology, Neoplatonism, and poetry). Even as I begin reimagining Narcissus, I am caught in an echo chamber where disputatious discourses resonate off of one another, creating polyphonic moments of harmony followed by the harshest of atonal discords.

Trapped, then, in an infinitely reflecting hall of mirrors, in an echoing text in which origins and ends are impossible to identify with confidence. Perhaps there is a "way out," a way beyond the reflective mirrorings; perhaps not. But, in any case, the type of mythic enclosure in which I have chosen to write will prove illuminating, though only darkly, for an undertaking that hopes to better understand the poetics of fictional texts, psychoanalysis, and subjectivity.

In the beginning is the mythic fiction, and a myth is a story that renews itself through interpretation. The myth of Narcissus—Narcissus refusing the cries of Echo; Narcissus longing to seize the image in the water; Narcissus changed into a flower—is one of the primordial myths of the late twentieth century. "Primordial," in this context, does not indicate a temporally distant but fixed origin of things; rather, following Carrin Dunne, "from *ar-,* which means 'to fit together,' we have the Latin *ordo,* order (originally a row of threads on a loom), and *ordiri,* to begin to weave, whence 'primordial' " (119). We are all woven into the fatal web of Narcissus.

A primordial myth is a woven web of meaning, a cultural text of behaviors and attitudes in which we are bound, but which also, and paradoxically, empowers us to speak. We speak of culture using figures of speech, and Western culture, to the extent that it is the descendant of Greek and European thought, lives within the boundaries of the text of narcissism. Whether the woven form of Narcissus will prove to be a mummy or a cocoon is a question not yet answerable.

Narcissus takes a slightly different shape depending upon the cultural genre—philosophy, literature, or psychoanalysis—in which he appears, but there is always reflection and self-reflexivity, the anxiety of death, and the inability to acknowledge the other (as the lover or as the world). In philosophy, René Descartes, in his *Meditations on First Philosophy* (1641), observed that if he wished to gain "firm and constant knowledge in the sciences, [he] would have to undertake, once and for all, to set aside all the opinions which [he] had previously accepted among [his] beliefs and start again from the very beginning" (17). Already the grandi-

osity inherent in a narcissistic position is apparent: Descartes feels he
must act "once and for all"; he must cast off "all" opinions and start again
"from the very beginning." Descartes, who should be numbered among
the great deconstructors of philosophy, founds modern philosophy because he fantasizes that he can be the maker of a mythless metaphysics,
ab initio and *ex nihilo.*

The founding act of modern philosophy, however, does not rest quite
on a nothing, but on a fragment of human experience, a kind of part-
object that is inflated into the basis both of certainty in the sciences and
of human identity as a *res cogitans,* a thinking thing. In the process of
formulating the *cogito,* Descartes is frightened by how easily he falls into
error. As he considers the untrustworthiness of his senses, using the
famous example of the wax, he complains that "even though I consider
all this in my mind without speaking, still *words* impede me, and I am
nearly deceived by the terms of *ordinary language*" (31; emphasis
added). Words interfere with the full immediacy of his indubitably true
relationship with his own thinking. It is not by "seeing" but by "judging"
that we say we "see the same wax" before and after it has been burned by
the candle.

Continuing his remarks on his powers of perception and the likeli-
hood that the senses will lead to error, Descartes invents a short fiction:
"So I may by chance look out of a window and notice some men
passing in the street, at the sight of whom I do not fail to say that I see
men, just as I say that I see wax; and nevertheless what do I see from
this window except hats and cloaks which might cover ghosts or automata which move only by springs?" (31). Apart from the fact that
Descartes indeed comes to argue for this very idea of the human body
as a machine[1]—what is initially the basis for doubt later becomes a
conclusion of his thinking—the images of "ghosts and automata" are
quite intriguing. The ghost is the return of that which we, apparently,
do not desire to return, and the automaton is one of Jacques Lacan's
central metaphors for narcissism.

In the construction of the subject that will ensure both self-identity
and epistemological veracity, Descartes constructs a subject severed
from the world and from its own body. It is a terribly dissociated subject
that he writes so eloquently. The I of the *cogito* is, of course, the subject

1. Descartes writes that "the human body may be considered as a machine so built and
composed of bones, nerves, muscles, veins, blood, and skin that even if there were no mind in
it, it would not cease to move in all the ways that it does at present when it is not moved under
the direction of the will, nor consequently with the aid of the mind, but only by the condition
of its organs" (80).

of theory; it is concocted by thinking so that theory can rest on a sure foundation. And although Descartes inscribes this abstract subject, this *res cogitans,* in the center of modernity, he also labors to create like-minded readers "who would want to meditate seriously along with me, and who are capable of freeing the mind from attachment to the senses and clearing it entirely of all sorts of prejudices" (11). Descartes, with the logic of narcissism, must exclude differences if the certain selfsame is to be achieved.

I am not much interested in epistemological certainty or such a purgation of the senses, but I am curious about how, after being cast out of the magic circle of the *res cogitans,* ghosts like the world and the body return. Descartes, of course, makes a rational provision for the return of materiality by detouring through his argument about the necessary existence of God as a perfect, and therefore trustworthy, being. But his radical subjectification of consciousness, followed by the loss of a context in which subjectivity could be grounded upon a belief in the existence of God, has generated the history of philosophical speculation from his period to our own. One attempt has followed another—from Kant through Hegel, Nietzsche, Marx, and Heidegger—to think beyond a solipsistic *cogito* toward a recovery of the body, other persons, and the world itself.

Lawrence Cahoone defines this philosophical narcissism as "subjectivism," or "the conviction that the *distinction between subjectivity and non-subjectivity is the most fundamental distinction*" (19). He contends that as long as a transcendent principle such as God, Logos, reason, or nature acted to connect the subject and the object, subjectivism could legitimately operate as a model of life in the world. Once these terms of transcendence are eroded, however, the subject becomes an emptiness to be filled by a world with the "status of mirror, sign, or representation of the self... a kind of depth-less surface" (83).

This "depth-less surface" describes quite precisely much of the structuralist and poststructuralist discussion about the world and about the entity *subjected* by the powers of the symbolic order of language and culture. Barthes, Lévi-Strauss, Foucault, Derrida, and Lacan announce the death of the individual, "man," or the author, the antiquated idea of the unified self, and its replacement by a subject that is divisively constituted by the ways that language "speaks itself."

Cahoone calls the narcissistic dialectic the "reduction of the existential integrity of the subject or the object," a movement that, since subject and object are no longer held *en rapport* by any transcendent "third thing," results in a "dichotomy of indistinguishables" (98), which is no dichotomy at all. Subject and object blend and merge into one another; everything becomes a part of an indivisible totality, a dead and unbroken mirror. Having jettisoned the noumenal "third thing," everything becomes appearance of appearance—Nietzsche has overthrown Plato and Kant—and Narcissus's image is indistinguishable from Narcissus himself. Narcissus exists just *as* a reflection, a simulacrum, on the barely rippling plane of the waters.

Whereas the threat of absolute solipsism marks the presence of Narcissus in philosophy, in literature, Narcissus's first and most abiding home,[2] his sign is the self-reflexivity of narrative. As Linda Hutcheon argues in *Narcissistic Narrative,* "the novel from its beginnings has always nurtured a self-love, a tendency towards self-obsession. Unlike its oral forbears, it is both the storytelling and the story told. Teiresias' warning about Narcissus' self-awareness is perhaps well directed *from the start:* he will live long, 'si se non noverit,' if he does not know himself" (10). Since its earliest manifestations, the novel has been aware of its own self-reflexive possibilities, has worked with a consciousness of what the Russian Formalists termed "baring the device": stripping bare the structural aspects of a story as it is being told and thereby acknowledging fiction as an artificial construct, even when the fiction poses as mimetically "real."

Citing *Tristram Shandy, Don Quixote,* and *Jacques le fataliste,* to which I would add even earlier works such as Apuleius's *Golden Ass* and Petronius's *Satyricon,* Hutcheon observes that "one might choose to see the origins of this phenomenon [the novel's early self-consciousness] in the parodic intent of the novel, in the unmasking of dead conventions by a mirroring of them" (10). But the mirror distorts—it refracts the light of reflection—so as to allow us to see social conventions, and even death itself, with a keener eye.

The mirror of fiction does not, in other words, naively and mimetically reflect its subject matter. Rather, fiction transforms the writer, the reader, and society by a critical unmasking of the forms of death. Such an unmasking is at least implicitly synonymous with an offering of an alternative to the "dead conventions" that often govern social interaction as well as the "interior" lives of individuals. One must reflectively gaze at death before there is a possibility of becoming more free in the face of

2.   For a thorough recapitulation of the Narcissus theme in literature between the classical writers and the nineteenth century, see Louise Vinge's *The Narcissus Theme in Western European Literature up to the Early Nineteenth Century.*

the glassy-eyed stare of Thanatos. (Needless to say, such a liberation is always partial, and reading, like psychoanalysis, is interminable.)

Michael Boyd, speaking of the modernist self-reflexive novel and its successors among the *nouveau roman* and postmodernist works, makes a similar connection:

> Fiction that looked at itself, that was reflexive, would not be creating yet another fictional world that needed to be related to the "real" world: it would take as its "object" the *relationship* between "real" and fictional worlds.... Call it metafiction. Or call it the relexive novel, the novel about the novel—onanistically or perhaps incestuously using its own imaginative energy to sustain itself. (23)

Boyd later adds that such acts as "suicide" and "masturbation" are necessarily self-reflexive (36). Suicide, incest, and masturbation—all are brought into the closest conjunction within the modern narcissistic novel (where, in the library of Borges, Leopold Bloom sits in the tub while Quentin Compson stares out across the iron gray waters of the Charles).

Literary theory followed, and now contributes to, the self-reflexive character of the novel. If there is nothing but language, which erases the author, and all language is self-referential, then "we" are irrevocably enmeshed within the nets of a narcissistic practice. If all discourse is ultimately self-reflexive and nonreferential, and if the subject is constituted by language, then the subject is a poetic entity. Since the linguistic turn in many areas of thought, there has developed an acute consciousness of the textual metaphoricity of the subject, the subject as a field of metaphor, illusion, fiction, and myth.

Jacques Derrida, with an eye toward Narcissus, has written of the connection between subjectivity and the ruses of metaphor: "The specular dispossession which at the same time institutes and deconstitutes me is also a law of language. It operates as a power of death in the heart of living speech: a power all the more redoubtable because it opens as much as it threatens the possibility of the spoken word" (*Of Grammatology,* 141; hereafter cited as G). Mirrors, textual or otherwise, simultaneously grant temporary identity and "dispossess" us, break us into incomprehensible fragments.

A text is a form of the articulated psyche, psyche manifested as narrative. From this perspective, psyche and text are metaphorical

correlates—each can be seen in terms of the other—because "the structure of literature *is* in some sense the structure of mind" (Brooks, 4); or,
as Ragland-Sullivan comments in her "prolegomena" to a Lacanian poetics, "literature operates a magnetic pull on the reader because it is an
allegory of the psyche's fundamental structure" (381).

George Steiner has phrased it even more succinctly: "meaning," he
remarks, "is animate formality" (4). When reading texts or the self poeti-
cally, both the "animate" and the "formal" qualities must be taken into
account. Because psyche can be seen as text, it requires a hermeneutical
"reading"; because each text is a narrative formalization of psyche, psychoanalysis can be a useful tool for the hermeneutical task.

Such a claim can be made of psyche and text only if metaphoricity is
already operating, allowing us to see one thing *as* another, to see psyche
as if it were a text and to see a text as if it were a form of psyche. To step
outside of this metaphorical viewpoint—for instance into the perspective that treats psyche as the result of neuronal connections or a text as
only a rule-governed arrangement of signs—is always possible and often
desirable, but there is always a loss as well.

Although any perspective, in sum, is a kind of imaginative schema,
different fields imply vastly different practices, assumptions of truth and
research, and different operative metaphors. All may be, in some sense,
understood as "text," but all "texts" are not the same. In each interpretive perspective, in other words, a spectrum of the literal and the figural
is constructed, usually unconsciously and on the level of culture rather
than individuality. Meaning, as Lévi-Strauss reminds us, is transferred not
from term to term but from code to code—that is, from a category or
class of terms to another category or class. It would be particularly
erroneous to assume that one of these classes or categories naturally
pertains to literal meaning and the other to figurative meaning, for these
functions are interchangeable and relative to each other. The function of
each class is initially undetermined; then, according to the role that it
will be called upon to play in a global structure of signification, it induces the opposite function in the other class (*The Jealous Potter,* 194;
hereafter cited as JP). When we do choose to shift points of view, we also
lose the power that a particular metaphorical conjunction gives us to
respond to questions such as how psyche and text are similar or dissimilar, or what the boundaries of such a metaphor might be. We always find
ourselves within the field of one metaphor or another; our thinking is
always rife with the illusions entailed by symbolization, fantasy, or art.

This "lie"—the structure of which can be read as mythicity, fantasy, the imaginal, or narrativity—is central to my investigation of the figurations that Narcissus takes on in philosophy, psychoanalysis, and fiction, because human thinking itself is necessarily a composition of truth and falsehood. There is no absolute knowing, though this "as if" position can be imaginatively maintained for an extended period; we must, therefore, acquaint ourselves with the multitudinous ways in which we trick ourselves into beliefs about the world, subjectivity, or texts. As John Fowles has scribbled in a reflexive memo to himself: "You are not the 'I' who breaks into the illusion, but the 'I' who is part of it" ("Notes," 167).

Kant was "the first to teach us to regard illusion as a necessary structure of thought about the unconditioned. The transcendental *Schein* is not mere error, a pure accident in the history of thought; it is a *necessary illusion*" (Ricoeur, 529). Illusion is a necessary structure of thought about the conditioned world as well, and I am in pursuit of this illusion—this persistent mirage in the waters of representation—through the psychoanalytic and the fictional perspectives on narcissism.

The depths and heights of a mythically narrated, cosmological perspective are transformed by contemporary human sciences into surface and gap; the invisible becomes visible (all is *phainomena* in Heidegger's sense, brought into manifestation in the light of day); and the spirit (of the writer and of God) becomes the body of the disseminated text. Words, like the psyche, become "alien, shattered like a broken pane of glass" (Sonoda, 234). Yet it is this very brokenness that induces speech and the desire for the other, both of which Narcissus resists.

The myth of Narcissus narrates a dialectic of reflection that is internally disturbed by an obsessive desire for immediacy. It is a poetic narrative that depicts a way of being that wants to destroy the surface of things, the appearances, in order to plunge into the depths and shatter the reflecting mirror completely so that the other of love—which is only apparently other—might be possessed. But a terrible paradox binds any desire that enters into this symbolic topos: If the appearances are destroyed, then the apparent object of love, the image of Narcissus, will also be destroyed. If, on the other hand, the mirror is not shattered, Echo will remain but a desolate voice, and Narcissus himself will die from the grief of love unreturned. How shall we respond to the mirror with which we are so closely identified? How shall we think about myth and the fictions of representation?

Lévi-Strauss, who once again will serve as a representative mythologist, writes that "with an authority that cannot be denied, it [mythic thinking] arises from the depths of time, setting before us a magnifying mirror that reflects, in the massive form of concrete images, certain mechanisms by which the exercise of thought is ruled" (JP, 206). Narcissus stands quite close to this "magnifying mirror" that from the "depths of time" reflects the invariant laws of the mind, an interesting correspondence—itself a mythical distinction—between surface and depth.

Myth, however, is no longer a term tantamount to "universal narrative," at least if the latter speaks of a ritual or narrative content supposedly found across time and cultures. If, as Mieke Bal argues, "a myth is a myth because, under the layers of dust of historically changing signifiers, it remains the same signifier-independent signified, a universal story" (59), then very few believe any longer in myth (which Bal claims enables the illusions of essentiality, objectivity, and eternity). There are, however, other ways of understanding the function of myth than as a naive universalism.

Eric Gould, in *Mythical Intentions in Modern Literature,* has made a penetrating and sustained examination of the relation between myth and universality in light of poststructuralism's insistence on language and the "letter" of the signifier. It is Gould who coined the term "mythicity," a notion that is central to my analysis of the structure of illusion inevitably encountered in any discussion of the textual subject.

Myth, Gould argues, cannot exist without an *"ontological gap between event and meaning."* He continues:

> A myth intends to be an adequate symbolic representation by closing that gap, by aiming to be a tautology. The absent origin, the arbitrary meaning of our place in the world, determines the mythic.... [Myth's] meaning is perpetually open and universal only because once the absence of a final meaning is recognized, the gap itself demands interpretation which, in turn, must go on and on, for language is nothing if it is not a system of open meaning. (6)

Because myth occurs as an event of language, it can never have a "final meaning" and can never remain identified with itself as an origin.

In the beginning is the gap; in the beginning were the gods, but the gods were established through divine autogenesis (perhaps the "oldest" expression of narcissism), through a split between the nothing of godhood and the something of the gods, or through strife between different generations of the gods. From the Vedas to Hesiod's *Theogony,* divinities originate in the myths, and there is always, necessarily, a "break" of some kind from the older, primeval unity of the universe.[3]

Philosophical discourse, like its mythological progenitors, also manifests an ineradicable sense of a gap or split in Being. The pre-Socratics worried about the relationship between the One and the Many; Plato labored to show how the Forms interact with the phenomenal world; Jewish and Christian theology theorized about the Fall; Kant asserted that though we may "think" the noumenal, we cannot "know" it; Kierkegaard emphasized the infinite gulf between the human and the divine; Nietzsche's philosophical hammerblows attacked the distinctions between the true and the false world; Heidegger discussed the "ontological difference" between Being and beings; and Derrida has developed the ideas surrounding the trace and *différance*. Psychoanalysis follows suit as it considers the splitting of the ego, part-objects, and the irruptions of the unconscious into the apparent unity of consciousness.

The gap, the *chaos* of the Greeks (from *chainein:* to gape), is an invariant, though multiformed, experience of human existence. Poststructuralism, then, has clearly not stumbled suddenly upon the gap, but it has brought the greatest intellectual pressure to bear on the gap as a manifestation of a *linguistic* rupture between language and meaning, between signifiers and signifieds. Fredric Jameson has written that the "attempt to see the literary work as a linguistic system is in reality the application of a *metaphor*" (viii); and analogously, poststructuralism's unrelenting focus on the ontological gap as an insoluble problem of language is also a metaphor. But for the purpose of hearing the speech of Narcissus in contemporary discourse, it is a good metaphor, for it takes us directly into the space of fiction or into that which Gould calls "mythicity."

Mythicity—which becomes synonymous with the necessary structures of illusion in psychoanalysis and fiction—is the consequence of the proposition that "myth is a *metaphysics of absence implicit in every sign*" (Gould, 195). It is not, as in some nonlinguistic definitions of myth, *mana,* or the numinous, an "aura surrounding some essential thing, not something instinctively known, but something discovered through a whole network of interpretation, in which the archetype and its discursive extension are not possible to differentiate" (32). Meanings are on the surface, texts to be read.

---

3. This begs the question of the relationship between the gods and the origins of the myths, of how the myths arose in response to a condition of having been addressed by divinity. A discussion of these matters would take me too far afield, but see, for instance, Heidegger's essay "Hölderlin and the Essence of Poetry" or Cassirer's *Language and Myth.*

Gould is arguing against those schools of myth interpretation in which myth was understood as a category of feeling, such as Cassirer's discussion, itself borrowed from the anthropologists and philologists, of *mana;* Rudolf Otto's presentation of the *mysterium tremendum;* or, and especially, Jung's work on the archetypes. Because these modernist interpreters of myth were still working within a basically Kantian framework, each retained some sense of a distinction between a transcendent reality and its manifestations in the phenomenal world. When this fundamental binary opposition collapses, the definition of myth as related to *mana* or its equivalents, without attention to the linguistic implications of this definition, also collapses.

Thinkers such as Jung and Cassirer, however, were not as naive about the centrality of language as some have claimed. Jung, for example, claimed that "myth is the primordial language natural to psychic processes [that are] best and most succinctly reproduced by *figurative language*" (*Psychology and Alchemy,* 25; emphasis added), and Cassirer's work on the dialectic between language and myth also remains illuminating. In fact, Cassirer could write that there is a common point of contact between language and myth, "for, no matter how widely the contents of myth and language may differ, yet the same form of mental conception is operative in both. It is the form which one may denote as *metaphorical thinking;* the nature and meaning of metaphor is what we must start with if we want to find, on the one hand, the unity of the verbal and the mythical worlds and, on the other, their difference" (84).[4] For both Jung and Cassirer, then, the study of myth leads naturally to a study of the imagination and metaphor.

But such earlier commentators also stressed the numinosity of myth, which was ultimately translinguistic in nature. The poststructuralists, on the other hand, focus entirely on the linguisticality of myth. This endeavor is a necessary and salutary response and one that makes discoveries that were literally invisible for its predecessors who were not trained in the rhetoric of signs. (Saussure had not yet become such a dominant figure in the debates of the human sciences.)

"Language," Gould argues, "embodies the semiotic gap which determines all interpretation, and myth is that function of language which intentionally tries to close that gap" (42). The logic of narcissism, which is a totalizing logic, tries to close that gap absolutely, with murder and suicide. Metaphor, as well as myth, is constructed around the gap, and

---

4. For another discussion of this relationship, which agrees with Cassirer that myth is not conflatable into linguistic models, see Albert Cook's *Myth and Language.*

"no metaphorical language confronts non-being quite so squarely and definitively as myth. Mythicity . . . is the condition of filling the gap with signs in such a way that Being continues to conceal Nothing as a predication of further knowledge" (43). The hidden presence of the nothing necessitates myth, metaphor, and endless interpretive play. But Narcissus refuses to see the insubstantial shadows, the shades of nothingness, that lie so close to his fixed and staring face.

Thus interpretation, when enacted in the hope of filling out the absence of complete meaning, tends toward a reenactment of a myth. Interpretation is a *circumambulatio* of text or psyche; it is an itinerant, peripatetic activity and not a destination of thought. Writing and thinking, then, cannot be understood as definition, but only as a slow and attentive stroll through the territory we call the world. (Socrates should have walked away from the city into the countryside more often—though perhaps with companions other than Ion.)

The idea of mythicity requires several qualifications. First, we are always involved in mythicity and its twin, metaphoric discourse. For instance, the "gap" of which Gould speaks is not an "objective" something in the world. It is not as if the gap were a hypostatized substance, present a priori, that is filled in with language as a crack in a stone wall is filled, and therefore "fixed," with cement. Myth attempts to "fill" the ineradicable abyss that opens within reflection and writing—or, to change images, to heal the wound that is the gap—but the gaping wound, which inheres within any discourse, is always reconstituted.

The semiotic gap serves synecdochically to represent the other forms of the gap mentioned above, which, to repeat myself, renders *différance* archetypal—a psychic and philosophical structure, not a content. Derrida would certainly reject such a suggestion, for "there is a *sure* play: that which is limited to the *substitution* of *given* and *existing, present,* pieces. In absolute chance, affirmation also surrenders itself to *genetic* indetermination, to the *seminal* adventure of the trace" ("Structure, Sign, and Play," 292; hereafter cited as SSP).

In calling *différance* archetypal, I am engaging in "sure" play that requires structure and a center (though not a center of presence). I am not convinced—since language as reading and writing is always bound to a truth and falsity of rhetoric, grammar, and tradition—that there is ever the "absolute chance" of which Derrida speaks so eloquently. Temporarily, it must suffice to observe that myth begets myth and metaphor begets metaphor, even in the form of a critique of myth, and that both birthing processes depend on likenesses as well as differences.

The second qualification also has to do with the ontological-semiotic gap, but this time apropos of the form of the "Nothing" that Gould discusses. "We have always been," he writes, "beings projected into Nothing, and for that reason there has always been myth. For it is first myth, and then, I would suggest, modern interpretation theory, that reminds us strongly today that without a sense of Nothing, there is no selfhood or freedom" (10). Both myth and contemporary hermeneutics, Gould suggests, emerge in response to the "Nothing."

Heidegger, whose presentation of *das Nichts* Gould is following, comments that "in the clear night of the nothing of anxiety the original openness of beings as such arises: that they are beings—and not nothing. But this 'and not nothing' we add in our talk is not some kind of appended clarification. Rather it makes possible in advance the revelation of beings in general. The essence of the originally nihilating nothing lies in this, that it brings Da-sein for the first time before beings as such" ("What is Metaphysics?" 105; hereafter cited as WM).

Mythicity is the awareness of the nothing in the midst of our textual discourses and of our existence itself. "Da-sein means: being held out into the nothing" (WM, 105). Myth, therefore, means speaking in response to the nihilating, which is not annihilation, of nothing. Reading and writing mean learning to pay homage to the nothing that dwells silently within texts; being a self means honoring finitude and its many gaps.

For Descartes, on the other hand—and again I note the nearness of his thought to narcissism—nothingness is nothing but a "deficiency" in the epistemological labor to gain truth. Since error self-evidently occurs— some believe their bodies are made of glass and the senses might translate a tree into a man—Descartes must develop an account of error that does not imply imperfection on God's part, since God is by definition the perfect being. When the philosopher gazes at his own thinking, he recognizes that in addition to the idea of God, there is also

> a certain negative idea of nothingness, or of what is infinitely removed from every kind of perfection. And I see that I am, as it were, a mean between God and nothingness . . . but if I consider myself as somehow participating in nothingness or not-being, that is, in so far as I am not myself the supreme being and am lacking many things, I find myself exposed to an infinity of defects, so that I should not be astonished if I go wrong. (52)

Nothingness is a privation of the perfect and therefore a source of error, but Descartes is unable to think more deeply into the nothingness because it is, as it were, a regulative concept that frees God from the taint of error and frees Descartes from allowing the nothing to threaten the full self-presence of the *res cogitans* to itself.

Idealism, intimately related to narcissism, underwent fundamental changes in the two centuries after Descartes; in particular, the "I" overtly replaced Descartes's confidence in the otherness of God as the final regulator of Being. "What has become of the horror?" asks Schopenhauer. "I am, nothing else exists; sustained by me, the world reposes, in the repose that emanates from me: How should it terrify me, how should its greatness amaze me, which is never anything but the measure of my own greatness, a greatness that always surpasses it!" (quoted in Blumenberg, 269). The voice of Narcissus has become magisterial.

But Schopenhauer's hammer-wielding disciple, Nietzsche, launched a scathing attack on idealism; Narcissus's voice, with its refusal of the horror of nothingness, gave way to the dithyrambs of the god who tears and is torn. In a prefiguration of Heidegger and the poststructuralists, Nietzsche announced the encounter with the nothing in the symbolic language of myth itself.

Dionysos, in *The Birth of Tragedy,* represented the nothing, while Apollo came to symbolize the mythopoeic activity of art and culture that veiled the abyss from the direct gaze of human sight through the necessary intermediary of representation. And yet Apollo and Dionysos, who shared the shrine at Delphi, are eternally engaged in a play of appearances that is the "world." The world of phenomenal appearance, as an artistic production, allows Dionysos to "perpetually entertain" (52) himself in the revelry of representation, which is but a dream of a dream. To the fatally playful *agōn* between Dionysos and Apollo, Nietzsche adds the human artist, writing that "only insofar as the genius in the act of artistic creation coalesces with this primordial artist of the world, does he know anything of the eternal essence of art; for in this state he is, in a marvelous manner, like the weird image of the fairy tale which can turn its eyes at will and behold itself; he is at once subject and object, at once poet, actor, and spectator" (*The Birth of Tragedy,* 52). The weird image of a fairy tale—or Narcissus, who within the shimmering mirage of reflection also longs to be both subject and object of his own desire. Against Nietzsche's intentions, Narcissus continues to resound through the music of Dionysos.

A microdeconstruction of Nietzsche's passage leads back into the midst of poststructuralism and the discussion of mythicity. In the contemporary milieu, it is no longer the "genius" but language itself that engages in the slippery play of the god of all wet and growing things; and the opposition between the "primordial author" and the human author, with the image of the authoritative writer and its echoes of Schopenhauer and Indian philosophy, is deconstructed into a network of signifiers whose rapid dance creates an incessant hum of significatory practices and possibilities. The ground of *Atman-Brahman* gives way to the groundlessness of *lila*. Once we have surrendered the truth of the noumenal world in itself that, though unknowable, nonetheless served the function of regulating and grounding the phenomenal, we become part of the reflectively reflexive world of Narcissus: subject and object, reader and writer, the literal and the figurative.

In his first *Critique,* Kant wrote that

> it does indeed follow that all possible speculative knowledge of reason is limited to mere objects of *experience.* But our further contention must also be duly borne in mind, namely, that though we cannot *know* these objects as things in themselves, we must yet be in position at least to *think* them as things in themselves; otherwise we should be landed in the absurd conclusion that there can be appearance without anything that appears. (27)

We have long ago entered the "absurd conclusion" and can now only consent to learn what absurdity means in its postmodern guise. The *Ding an sich* disappears in order for the phenomenon to appear as that which, as Heidegger states, "shows itself in itself," though this "showing-itself is not just any showing-itself, nor is it some such thing as appearing. Least of all can the Being of entities ever be anything such that 'behind it' stands something else 'which does not appear' " (*Being and Time,* 60).

Metaphysics becomes the description of the appearance of appearance, a phenomenology of the phenomenal. Writing only swirls the water of Narcissus's pool; the self, instead of an *imago dei* or a transcendental unity of apperception, becomes a reflecting reflection. Derrida summarizes this situation:

> Representation mingles with what it represents, to the point where one speaks as one writes, one thinks as if the represented were nothing more than the shadow or reflection of the representer. A dangerous promiscuity and a nefarious complicity between the reflection and the reflected which lets itself be seduced narcissistically. (G, 36)

"Seduced narcissistically." Rather than a hierarchy of signs that was common to the metaphysics of Plato and Descartes, all representations become part of textual play, polymorphously and perversely weaving among themselves the echo of meaning. But Echo, the voiced other of the myth, remains unheard and out of sight. Narcissus is busy with himself, dying for love.

Having clarified, however briefly, the gap inherent in texts and existence, surveyed Heidegger's thought of the nothing, and remembered that Nietzsche already knew that myth veils the turmoil of the abyss, we find ourselves in the circular mirror returning to the notion of mythicity. Mythicity is the way in which myth, and interpretation of myth, attempts to fill with significance the gap between event and meaning, between sign and referent, and between signifier and signified. But this "significance" itself is none other than a mythic or literary narrative (Gould uses Joyce, Eliot, and Lawrence as his case studies), which is also a chain, or entanglement of chains, of signifiers and signifieds. Signs answer signs.

But the sign/gap is read differently before and after the entrance into the era of the absurd. For Kant, the productive imagination, which stands as the mediator between sensibility and intelligibility, is the a priori necessity for any knowledge at all, but I prefer that the structure of the imagination not remain a purely formal criterion for the possibility of experience, a "blind but indispensable function of the soul" (Kant, 112). Instead, the imagery of Narcissus and the way such images illuminate specific novels as well as the fractured signifying of the textual subject will provide at least a dark sense of sight. Kant might claim that this moves us from the productive to the reproductive imagination, and therefore from transcendental philosophy to psychology. For us, this movement means that we have crossed a watershed of thought and must examine not the logic of critical philosophy but, to use Lacan's term, "reason after Freud."

When we enter into the domain of reason after Freud, we have left Descartes, if not behind, then at least in a very different symbolic space. For Descartes, reason is the power of self-transparent immediacy that provides proof of God's existence as well as the grounds for the clarity of scientific method. For psychoanalysis, reason is something altogether different, a difference that I will examine as I read through Freud to Lacan's comments on the Cartesian *cogito* (and thus, I take it, on the narcissism of idealism as a whole).

It is of course Freud who first introduces the term "narcissism" into psychoanalytic terminology, and in so doing he ipso facto renews the significance of the poetic myth of Narcissus. And as Hans Blumenberg observes, "the central mythical figures that Freud reintroduces into general circulation—Narcissus and Oedipus—are representative of the 'significance' of myth itself. For narcissism, too, is a turning back: a turning away from the reality outside the ego, an avoidance of the expenditure involved in separation and the energy involved in existence" (92). This "turning back" is the very essence of reflection for both Narcissus, who exhibits only a semblance of looking outward, and Descartes, as a representative of the tradition of subjective idealism.

Blumenberg believes that myths "represent a world of stories that localizes the hearer's standpoint in time in such a way that the fund of the monstrous and the unbearable recedes in relation to man" (117). Myths allay the unbearable anxiety of living in the truth of the "absolutism of reality," the realization that human beings, even in this age of the enframing grid of technology, do not control life and hold the powers of destruction at bay.

Descartes's myth, indeed the "fundamental myth" of idealism, operates by making the terror purely cerebral, and the "malevolent demon of Cartesian doubt is the monster of a prior world of terrors that are now definitively overcome" (Blumenberg, 267). The "zero point" of ultimate doubt—the question of certainty gives way to the question of personal existence—becomes the beginning point of an almost impregnable armature that defends the thinking thing, the subject, from the contingent horror of existence. Descartes can conclude as he sits "by the fire, wearing a winter dressing gown, holding this paper in [his] hands" (18), that whatever happens is simply a further assurance of his own consciousness. He forgets that the conjunction of paper and fire may ignite the unexpected.

This "unexpected," which psychoanalysis calls the unconscious, is the aperture into the nearly impregnable world of narcissism. In the sections on psychoanalysis, I concentrate on Freud's formulations of narcissism and on Lacan's proposals about the "mirror stage" of identity-formation and on his analyses of Narcissus as phantom and automaton. Lacan, reworking Freud, places us immediately in an arena where the power of language brings psychoanalysis and literature into the closest proximity.

The psychoanalysis of the logic of narcissism aids us in understanding how better to comprehend the fictive quality of subjectivity. The study then moves into the realm where textuality and the illusions of fiction are the most unconcealed, into literature itself, before returning in "Narcissus in the Theater of the Other" to a deconstruction of the logic of narcissism that occurs as a consequence of a reconstruction of the textual subject.

2

The Scar of Narcissus:
Sigmund Freud and the
Psychoanalysis of Narcissism

In the realm of fiction we find the plurality of lives we need.
—Sigmund Freud

With the work of Sigmund Freud, Narcissus is translated from the world of poetry into that of psychoanalysis. The clinical use of the term "narcissism" originated with Havelock Ellis, for whom it meant only an autoerotic sexuality, and passed through the hands of Paul Näcke, who coined the term *Narziβmus* in his comments on Ellis's research. Freud, in his turn, borrowed the word from Näcke and proceeded to transform it into one of the central concepts of psychoanalytic investigation, in which the language of object choices, ego instincts, and libidinal cathexes transplanted the language of poetry in which Narcissus had lived during the preceding centuries. The fundamental issues that mark the presence of Narcissus, however, remained very much the same, namely questions of love, self-reflection, and death.

Although Freud's 1914 essay "On Narcissism: An Introduction" provides his most detailed examination of narcissism, the term itself, as well as the complex of thoughts surrounding the term, makes its appearance in a number of Freud's other essays. In his "Three Essays on the Theory of Sexuality," first published in 1905, the term appears many times, but even though the essay certainly concerns itself with infantile sexuality and object choice, the material on narcissism per se is all inserted by Freud in 1915, a year after the publication of "On Narcissism."

In a brief recapitulation of the latter essay, Freud continues (in a paragraph that dates from 1920) to disparage Jung for "watering down" the libido theory and to state his earlier opinion that the "narcissistic or ego-libido seems to be the great reservoir from which the object-cathexes are sent out and into which they are withdrawn once more; the narcissistic libidinal cathexis of the ego is the original state of things, realized in earliest childhood, and is merely covered by the later extrusions of libido, but in essentials persists behind them" (*Three Essays,* 84). In this context, Freud admits that to speak of this "originary" kind of narcissism—and Narcissus brings with him a concern for origins, indeed a myth of origins that is a fantasy of autogenesis—is to "look across a frontier, which we may not pass" (84). As is his usual custom, Freud continues to push at the boundaries of the knowable.

Nonetheless, the first mention of narcissism, according to Laplanche and Pontalis, does in fact occur in the "Three Essays," but only in a footnote added in 1910 in which Freud speaks of "inverts" who "identify themselves with a woman and take *themselves* as their sexual object" (11n). Already, even at this early, inchoate phase of Freud's thinking on narcissism, object choice and the processes of identification are linked together.

Also in 1910, a few months after the "Three Essays," Freud published *Leonardo da Vinci and a Memory of His Childhood.* In this piece of psychoanalytic interpretation, Freud relates Leonardo's early childhood experiences—especially the famous fantasy in which Leonardo "remembered" a vulture descending into his cradle and striking its tail against his lips—to his adult character, with its artistic and scientific preoccupations, his coterie of beautiful male students, his inability to finish his paintings, and so forth. Narcissism receives only one mention, and a passing one at that. Freud comments that one type of homosexual "finds the objects of his love along the path of *narcissism,* as we say; for Narcissus, according to the Greek legend, was a youth who preferred his own reflection to everything else and who was changed into a lovely flower of that name" (50).

Although the term itself is not directly elaborated upon, the concept it represents nevertheless plays a central role in Freud's analysis of da Vinci, for his interpretation rests on the hypothesis that a boy like Leonardo "represses his love for his mother: he puts himself in her place, identifies himself with her, and takes his own person as a model in whose likeness he chooses the new objects of his love" (50). In fact, Freud concludes, although the boy becomes a homosexual, the "true" love object is the self. Thus, Freud arrives at the autoerotic object, and an incipient understanding of narcissism.

In 1911, in his essay on *Senatspräsident* Schreber, Freud analyzes the "part played by a homosexual wish in the development of paranoia" ("Psychoanalytic Notes," 163) and treats narcissism as a stage of development between autoerotism and object love. At the narcissistic stage, the only sexual object is the person's own ego, and Freud deduces that paranoiacs are fixated at the narcissistic stage, a stage prior to homosexual identification as well as heterosexual object love.

Later in this discussion, Freud remarks that his investigation of Schreber has led him into a series of observations about other psychological phenomena, notably schizophrenia. This is of interest not only because of its inherent importance but also because schizophrenia is Jung's "territory" more than it is Freud's, who tends to deal almost exclusively with neurotics. In the Schreber essay, Freud speaks of Jung's "extraordinary analytic acumen" (180), but this evaluation has drastically shifted by 1914, when "On Narcissism" is composed, in large part to refute Jung's challenge to Freud's theory of the libido. About the connection between narcissism and schizophrenia made during his analysis of Schreber—actually of his written memoirs—Freud writes that "regression travels back not merely to the stage of narcissism (manifesting itself in the shape of megalomania) but to a complete abandonment of object-love and to a restoration of infantile auto-erotism" (180).

Freud carries over much the same idea of narcissism into *Totem and Taboo* (1912–13), but in this book the idea is enlarged to fit not only neurotics and psychotics but also the animistic stage of humankind's evolution. In a gesture reminiscent of Jung (to whom he expresses his methodological indebtedness in the preface) and anticipating Erich Neumann's version of the history of consciousness, Freud writes:

> If we may take the now established omnipotence of thought among primitive races as a proof of their narcissism we may venture to compare the various evolutionary stages of man's conception of the universe with stages of the libidinous evolution of the individual. We find that the animistic phase corresponds in time as well as in content with narcissism, the religious phase corresponds to that stage of object finding which is characterized by dependence on the parents, while the scientific stage has its full counterpart in the individual's stage of maturity where, hav-

ing renounced the pleasure principle and having adapted himself
to reality, he seeks his object in the outer world. (117)

Without evaluating the anthropological validity of Freud's proposition, let me note only two things. First, the process of psychic evolution
goes, as it were, from the inside out: from the narcissistic self-cathexis of
the primitives through a dependent stage of object relations and finally
to a mature and clear-sighted adaptation to the external world. The
external world carries a greater ontological weight than the internal—
from autoerotism through the parental imago to the "real" object—and,
as the corollary proposition, the pleasure principle ("I want to love
myself and live in a fantasy of omnipotence") gives way to the reality
principle, which involves an acceptance of the limits of thought and of
others who exist outside of the system of an individual's fantasies. In the
great evolutionary narrative, Narcissus is for the most part superseded
by other figures of thought such as Oedipus, but, as Freud observes, "the
narcissistic organization is never altogether given up again" (116). Even
when we become "mature," there remain vestiges of self-absorption and
the pleasure principle at work in the psyche and, by implication, in the
social network in which the individual exists. In addition, the question
naturally arises: What "stage" follows the scientific?

My second gloss on the above passage is that Freud is, as usual, speaking metaphorically, but in the language of anthropology and psychoanalysis. These discourses rest on a mythological foundation (though "foundation" creates an erroneous impression of solid ground); or, to borrow
from Lévi-Strauss, they subsist on a particular psychic and textual
mythologem *and* upon the general operations of the mind that Lévi-
Strauss has explored.

Mythic thought operates, according to Lévi-Strauss, whenever "the
mind asks itself what signification is" (JP, 13), which of course includes
the activity of psychoanalysis.[1] Freud enacts a mythic mode of thought
and thereby creates a significatory space for a far wider range of interpretation than was available before his work. When Freud leaps from the

1.   Lévi-Strauss has a great deal to say about psychoanalysis and its relation to myth. See, for
instance, the chapter in *Structural Anthropology* on shamanism and the efficacy of symbols,
and the chapter in *The Jealous Potter* on "A Jivaro Version of *Totem and Taboo.*" In a word,
myths for Lévi-Strauss operate as a kind of metacode, a bundle of various codes of significance,
whereas psychoanalysis deciphers only the code of psychosexuality. Lévi-Strauss also rejects
Freud's evolutionism and regards "magic" and "science" as "two parallel modes of acquiring
knowledge" (*Savage Mind,* 13).

evolution of the individual to the evolution of the species, he is engaging in the kind of metaphorical translations from one code to another that are characteristic of mythic thinking, a cognition that relies on seeing resemblances in those things that are apparently dissimilar. In his system of thought at this juncture in his career, animism is the racial correlative of narcissism in the individual.

Animism, characterized by magical thinking and omnipotence of thought, is the initial evolutionary phase, which is followed by the religious and the scientific ones. In these latter stages, the omnipotence of thought steadily decreases in importance, although Freud admits that even science, in its "reliance upon the power of the human spirit" (*Totem and Taboo,* 115), retains a fragment of omnipotent thinking. The omnipotence of thought inherent in animism and narcissism, as Freud observes in a footnote, also "operates in the savage to make him refuse to recognize death as a fact" (117 n. 28). Narcissus longs for an immortal possession of himself, and death, unseen and unacknowledged, steals up to him and carries him down to Hades. The refusal of death is the refusal of the other; death's acknowledgment is, conversely, the recognition of the other.

Science has only retained a fragment of magical thinking; in fact, "only in one field," Freud continues, "has the omnipotence of thought been retained in our own civilization, namely in art. In art alone it still happens that man, consumed by his wishes, produces something similar to the gratification of those wishes, and this playing, thanks to artistic illusion, calls forth effects as if it were something real" (118). Artistic play, then, is related to narcissism because it exhibits omnipotence of thought ("I, the artist, can create my own world"), because it inevitably entails an animism (one thing constantly changes into another, as in the *Metamorphoses* or *Finnegans Wake*), and because art creates "real" effects through its illusions (like a neurosis, like a dream, like an idea). The illusory and the fantastic become, mysteriously, the basis of the real. This is art's "magic." In this respect, psychoanalysis is a form of art that provides, in D. W. Winnicott's phrase, a "transitional play space" in which reality and illusion can meet to further the creation of a self.

In *Group Psychology and the Analysis of the Ego* (1921), Freud uses his findings in both "On Narcissism" and *Totem and Taboo* to consider the problems inherent in the behavior of groups. He speaks of the distribution of narcissistic libido while the individual is in the state of "being in love" and of how the ego ideal becomes the "heir to the original narcissism in which the childish ego enjoyed self-sufficiency" (42). He concludes that a group—his examples are the army and the Catholic church—maintains its power because "a number of individuals . . . have put one and the same object in the place of their ego ideal and have consequently identified themselves with one another in their ego" (48).

But Freud admits that this mechanism, of itself, does not explain the "regressive" aspects of group behavior, and for an explanation he returns to the idea of the primal horde that he presented in *Totem and Taboo.* In that book he had argued that by idealizing and then murdering a common "father," the group (of men) becomes a bonded, homoerotic community of brothers. In *Group Psychology* he describes how the "primal father is the group ideal, which governs the ego in the place of the ego ideal" (58). The leader of the group—Freud suggests that the *Übermensch* is a figure of the distant past, not of the future—may retain an absolute narcissism, while collecting, as it were, the narcissistic energy of his followers.

In the postscript to *Group Psychology* Freud—now writing under the influence of Otto Rank rather than Jung—makes a very intriguing observation about the poet and poetry. He informs his readers that it is now "possible to specify the point in the mental development of mankind at which the advance from group psychology [the first psychology] to individual psychology was achieved also by the individual members of the group" (67), but to do so, he must return to the "scientific myth" of the father of the primal horde.

Once the group bands together to kill the father, they all "renounce their father's heritage" in order to coexist as a more or less equal band of brothers. This renunciation, which is a social equivalent of the castration complex and will reappear under the guise of the symbolic and the Name-of-the-Father in Lacan's theories, allows "individuality" to be transferred from the father-chief to each of the brothers. There are now a number of fathers instead of simply one, and each father shares in the power once held by the single ruler. The cut and scattered father—one of his names is Dionysos—is reconstituted as a group of individuals who, through totemic prohibitions, both "preserve and expiate the memory of the murder" (67).

"It was then," Freud continues, "that some individual, in the exigency of his longing, may have been moved to free himself from the group and take over the father's part. He who did this was the first epic poet; and the advance was achieved in his imagination" (68). The poet, in an artistic *Aufhebung,* recapitulates the primal father. This repetition and new creation do not occur in the person of the poet at the literal level of deeds—that divine act belongs only to the "original" father—but in the text of the epic poem about the hero.

At this stage, Orpheus the Lyre Player replaces Dionysos the Scattered, and instead of a "real" murder there is only metaphor: the poetic enactment of a ritual slaying. Thus the poet "creates the first ego ideal and the transition to the hero was probably afforded by the youngest son, the mother's favorite" (68). The process of substitution that is intrinsic to Freud's view of symbolization and symptom-formation is well under way in this 1921 depiction of the primal horde. The literal son becomes the poet, and his creation, the hero; the father becomes the totemic monster slain by the hero and then, eventually, the ego ideal. The son's journey to the place of the father occurs through substitution and displacement; it occurs, in other words, through a journey of metaphor and metonymy.

One gains identity by a practice of tropology, by the endless process of making art. In Julia Kristeva's succinct observation: "The subject is in process." And, as Freud writes, "the myth is the step by which the individual emerges from group psychology" (68). But such a separation is not equivalent to complete isolation, which would mean death, for the poet "is nevertheless able (as Rank has further observed) to find his way back to it [the group] in reality" (68).

The poet, who is the representative individual, returns to the social matrix by *telling* his disguised autobiography, the myth of the hero. This return, however, would not be possible without a certain kind of precondition on the part of the poet's audience: that is, an ability to identify with the hero precisely because the members of the audience have "the same relation of longing towards the primal father" (69) as the poet does. The person of the poet is inconsequential to the public, except that he is, in Blanchot's phrase, the necessary "site of narration"; the public desires only that their own stories be told and that they be allowed to enact the death of the father in the person of the epic hero.

Thus, the identity of the poet and the people follows from a reciprocal relationship, and both find the truth of their identity in the recited poem, which is itself a field of metaphorical and metonymical strife. Identity does not rest in a single, but in at least a double, place—Lacan speaks about the double foci of the *ellipse* along which the subject orbits—and is constructed as the in-between of an artwork. Since such textual-psychic making is possible only through the "third term" of the imagination, immediacy and absolute self-possession become impossible wishes. Narcissus, wanting to collapse the space of likeness and difference from which art emerges, is bound to die from the frustration that he cannot *make* anything, including love.

The postscript to *Group Psychology,* which I have analyzed in such detail, is a text—and a rather unexpected one—in which the concerns about narcissism, art, and identity come into direct contact with one another. In *The Ego and the Id*—the work in which Freud formalizes the structural theory of the mind as the ego, id, and superego—he more thoroughly defines primary and secondary narcissism and shows how the object instincts are sublimated through the intercession of the ego. "It may be said," he writes, "that this transformation of an erotic object-choice into an alteration of the ego is also a method by which the ego can obtain control over the id and deepen its relations with it—at the cost, it is true, of acquiescing to a large extent in the id's experiences. When the ego assumes the features of the object, it is forcing itself, so to speak, upon the id as a love-object and is trying to make good the id's loss by saying: 'Look, you can love me too—I am so like the object'" (20).

Speaking about the vicissitudes of the object choices once the object of love is lost, Freud remarks that the ego is "a precipitate of abandoned object-cathexes and it contains the history of those object-choices" (19), a statement which is congruent with his explorations in "Mourning and Melancholia," where he suggests that the lost object is reinstalled in the ego in the process of grieving.

When the object choice is renounced, the ego, through a process of identification, takes on the guise of the object so that it becomes the beloved of the id. This, however, is a falsified ego, a chameleon-ego that changes faces to meet the demands of the id in their secret and internalized love affair. From this perspective, the autoerotism of the narcissistic self is nonetheless a dyadic relationship, a kind of ersatz intersubjectivity founded on the ruins of the loss of the original object (the "mother").

The original object, cathected by the id before the ego was sufficiently formed to make any choice at all, is reclaimed by the ego once it has become strong enough to assert its rights. This reclamation, this installment of the already-fragmented object within the domain of the ego itself, is also the primary moment of self-creation, of the construction of personal identity. The mother-child unity is broken, and at that moment, however extensive the "moment" may be, the image of the love object is simultaneously fragmented and incorporated into the ego as part of the ego. The subject does not rise out of the ruins like a phoenix from the ashes; the ruins are constitutive of the self as a psychic organization.

The devastating loss of the other—who was not known as other but only as a mirror, as an extension of that which is mine—is compensated for by the establishment of the other as part of the self. "Love me, for I am so like the object." Now that the ego is divided, otherness can be recognized as such, for I am henceforth constituted by otherness. I am able to know the other because, paradoxically, I am the other even though I also remain not-other, myself.[2]

There is loss and there is gain. The loss is of the object and of the experience (Dionysian for Nietzsche, polymorphously perverse for Freud) of the world-self unity; the gain is that the process of building personal identity is initiated. The "self" that ensues will necessarily be a false self—it is constructed through identification of a fragmented object that is unavoidably misconstrued by the nascent ego—and will therefore be in need, eventually, of dismantling in the name of love.

To return to the text of *The Ego and the Id*: Freud notes that "the transformation of the object-libido into narcissistic libido which thus takes place obviously implies an abandonment of sexual aims, a desexualization—a kind of sublimation" (20). The sexual libido is redirected toward the ego, and the wound of the loss is covered over by, in Lacan's phrase, the "monumental construct of . . . narcissism" (*Ecrits*, 40; hereafter cited as E). This narcissistic organization is, ideally, broken apart by the development of the Oedipal triangle, but it can never be completely dissipated if a coherent self wishes to continue to exist within the conditioned world.

But the narcissistic organization of the self that covers the rupture of original unity with the object—although, technically, there can be no true "object" at this stage—also leads through melancholia toward another end: writing. Kristeva captures this moment of transition when she remarks that the "child-king becomes irremediably sad before proffering his first words: it is being separated from his mother, despairingly, with no going back, that decides him to try and recuperate her, along with other objects, in his imagination and, later, in words. If," she continues,

---

2. Freud says much the same thing in "The Unconscious" when he is discussing how it is possible for us to be conscious of other people:

> By the medium of consciousness each one of us becomes aware only of his own states of mind; that another man possesses consciousness is a conclusion drawn by analogy from the utterances and actions we perceive him to make, and it is drawn in order that this behavior of his may become intelligible to us. (It would probably be psychologically more correct to put it thus: that without any special reflection we impute to everyone else our own constitution and therefore also our consciousness, and that this identification is a necessary condition of understanding in us.) (102)

Identification by likeness is eventually balanced by a knowledge of difference, and the "intelligible" narrative about others by a sense of the ways in which narratives are broken and discontinuous.

"there exists no writing that is not amorous, then neither does there exist an imagination that is not, manifestly or secretly, melancholic" ("Melancholic Imaginary," 105; hereafter cited as MI).[3] This constellation of self-construction, narcissism, melancholy, and the writing imagination will stay with us throughout the examination of fiction and the textuality of the self, but for the time being, I want to remain within the Freudian corpus and move from *The Ego and the Id* to *Beyond the Pleasure Principle*.

Speaking of the short-lived "efflorescence" of infantile sexuality, Freud writes that "loss of love and failure leave behind them a permanent injury to self-regard in the form of a narcissistic scar" (14), a scar that leads to the sense of self-inferiority so common among neurotics. If we follow the line of development that I sketched above in relation to *The Ego and the Id,* then this "scar" does not occur *after* the ego is formed (as if there were a whole ego that is not wounded by the loss of love with its ensuing scar), but *as* the ego is being formed. The narcissistic scar is as integral to the subject's identity as Odysseus's scar on his thigh is to his own life history. It is a token of recognition; it is the "always already" of any psychic life. The foundational scar is the sine qua non of the trajectory of the ego's course.

Freud's discussion lays the groundwork for a rejection of the pleasure principle's primacy because of his discoveries about the role of repetition within traumatic neuroses as well as within the psyches of normal people whose lives, as they perceive them, are "pursued by a malignant fate or possessed by some 'daemonic' power" (15).[4] Freud is particularly interested in such experience when it is passive and the individual apparently exerts no influence over the staging of the repetitious event. As is so often the case, he turns to literature for his primary examples, remarking that

> the most moving poetic picture of a fate such as this is given by Tasso in his romantic epic *Gerusalemme Liberata.* Its hero, Tancred, unwittingly kills his beloved Clorinda in a duel while she is disguised in the armor of an enemy knight. After her burial he makes his way into a strange magic forest which strikes the Crusaders' army with terror. He slashes with his sword at a tall tree;

3.   I am reminded of Stephen Dedalus's relation to his mother and to words in *A Portrait of the Artist as a Young Man.*

4.   For one example of a literary manifestation of repetition and trauma, see Ernest Hemingway's "A Way You'll Never Be."

but blood streams from the cut and the voice of Clorinda, whose soul is imprisoned in the tree, is heard complaining that he has wounded his beloved once again. (16)

Tancred twice harms his beloved, both times when she is "not herself," when she is in disguise. What fate must await the ego when it disguises itself, when it becomes "like the object" in order to be loved by the dark face of the id? The knight slashes at the tree, and when the blood flows, Clorinda's voice is heard. The wound enables the voice to speak; the narcissistic construct of the ego enables the move into the symbolic.

Clorinda's imprisonment in a tree echoes Daphne's transformation in the face of Apollo's desire—perhaps, like Tancred's, an unconscious desire to destroy—and takes us back, repetitiously, to the Ovidian topos where Narcissus peers over the pond. Literature, with its intertextual and recurring topoi and mythoi, does, perhaps, lend its support to Freud's newly discovered aspect of psychic life, that is, "that there really does exist in the mind a compulsion to repeat which overrides the pleasure principle . . . something more primitive, more elementary, more instinctual than the pleasure principle" (16–17). At least that is what he apparently presumes, linking psychic life directly with the life of a text, in citing Tasso.

Although literature has been traditionally associated with its double task of "pleasing and instructing," its repetitive aspect—the way, for example, Narcissus appears in texts from a variety of periods and cultures—may be a type of compulsion more closely related to death, at least in our tendency to regress toward an earlier state. But what such a death instinct has to do with the writing and reading of texts must wait for further elaboration. Although death's face can always be discerned in the lines of a literary text, it is not only a death *instinct* shown there, but also death "raised" from instinct to the level of reflection through the cultural practices of love, art, and hermeneutics. Narcissus desires a *direct* reflection that does not pass through the third term of artistic reflection and is therefore fatally bound to the dualistic instincts of Eros and Thanatos, an entwinement from which there is no exit.

But before we make a final determination of Narcissus's fate, we must, finally, enter the text of Freud's "On Narcissism: An Introduction," an essay written largely in response to Jung's *Symbols of Transformation,* with its monistic theory of the libido. Freud's essay is a psychoanalytic meditation on love and its many vicissitudes, in the tradition of Plato's

Symposium or Augustine's *Confessions.*[5] To speak of love is to invoke
Eros and "merciless Aphrodite," those divinities whose presence inevitably brings pain to mortals, but whose absence brings an even greater
pain; or, as Freud translates from poetic language into the conceptual
idiom of psychoanalysis: "A strong egotism is a protection against disease, but in the last resort we must begin to love in order that we may
not fall ill, and must fall ill if, in consequence of frustration, we cannot
love" ("On Narcissism," 42; hereafter cited as N).

Since Freud composes a psychoanalytic, rather than a poetic or religious essay on love, he necessarily examines the stages of construction
of the love object, the types of love objects, and the psychic mechanisms
that either enable or obstruct us in the process of loving. But "On
Narcissism" deepens and systematizes the ideas that Freud had previously only touched upon cursorily. The essay begins by referring to the
received uses of the word. The first, which he draws from Näcke, is that
of a sexual "perversion" that characterizes one who experiences pleasure by gazing at and caressing his own body. In the second sense,
narcissism "would not be a perversion, but the libidinal complement to
the egoism of the instinct of self-preservation, a measure of which may
justifiably be attributed to every living creature" (31). Contemporary
analysis situates its debate about neurotic, psychotic, and healthy narcissism between these two poles.

Even at the very outset, "narcissism" is an ambiguous term, full of
ambivalences and semantically stretched. It will, in the course of the
essay, become more so. Freud, always a conscientious and meticulous
laborer, does not yet know the exact nature of the phenomenon that he
is dealing with, but he is aware of one of the central questions around
which the essay is organized: "What is the fate of the libido when withdrawn from external objects in schizophrenia?" (32). This is the question posed by Jung, and in order to respond to his pupil's challenge to his
libido theory, Freud enters new analytic territory.

When Freud, who had previously worked primarily with hysterics and
obsessional neurotics, turns to schizophrenia and paranoia (conditions
he calls paraphrenia), he is intrigued by the fact that these patients
exhibit two fundamental characteristics: "They suffer from megalomania
and they have withdrawn their interest from the external world" (31).
The two conditions go hand in hand. When libido is withdrawn from the
world, it is redirected upon the ego, and megalomania, a kind of magnifi-

---

5. Freud, in fact, cites the *Symposium* in *Beyond the Pleasure Principle* in support of his
"myth" of sexual origins.

cation of the ego, arises. In Freud's sense of the precisely calibrated hydraulics of the psyche, the one act necessarily results in the other, and narcissism as a neurotic or psychotic condition develops.

Freud comments that this narcissism, which he calls "secondary narcissism," is only an "exaggeration" or a "plainer manifestation" of something that "had already existed previously" (32). The psychological a priori, the basis from which an ego identity arises, is the "primordial" autoerotic instinct. It is at this primary and primordial level—and recall Dunne's etymology of "primordial" that I discussed in my introduction—where the narcissistic scar occurs. Primary narcissism is not just an enormous reservoir of libido waiting to be cathected onto objects; it is a wound.

Autoerotism has, like narcissism itself, both a developmental aspect and a structural aspect. In addition to being a stage preceding narcissism, for which there must be at least a partly unified ego, autoerotism also means a "sexual excitation which is generated and gratified at the same site in the case of each individual erotogenic zone" (Laplanche and Pontalis, 46). For autoerotism as an "early state of the libido" to become secondary narcissism, Freud argues that "some new operation in the mind" (34) must occur.

Although Freud begins his essay with a question about the libidinal attachments of schizophrenics, he soon moves far from his starting point in his attempt to understand narcissism. Children and primitives are among the first groups to come under his analytic gaze. These provide, Freud claims, evidence for an "original libidinal cathexis" (33). Primitives, from Freud's perspective, suffer from "an over-estimation of the power of wishes and mental processes, the 'omnipotence of thoughts,' a belief in the magical virtue of words, and a method of dealing with the outer world—the art of 'magic'—which appears to be a logical application of these grandiose premises" (32). Children's understanding of the external world, in sum, is analogous to that of the primitives.

Freud, of course, has his own kind of belief in the power of words, but more interestingly, he himself seems to be engaged in a kind of analogical thinking that we usually associate with primitives, children, psychotics, or poets. Children are like primitives are like schizophrenics; all exhibit narcissistic features. Even the images of narcissism become metaphorical, almost flamboyant. Object cathexes, writes Freud, are like the pseudopods of protoplasm; they are "emanations" of the libido.

Freud soon leaves such overt metaphors and returns to the analytic mode of speech to differentiate object libido from ego libido. The highest form of an object cathexis, Freud claims, is being in love, whereas the paranoiac's fantasy of the "end of the world," in which the libido may either flow onto the loved object or back upon the ego, is the opposite condition. Apocalypticism, megalomania, and narcissism form a triadic phenomenon; or, perhaps better, they represent a series of different images for the same phenomenon. Abel Tiffauges, the protagonist of Tournier's *The Ogre,* will show us more about this intersection.

Freud insists on these distinctions for at least four reasons. First, his analyses of the transference neuroses had led him to such a necessity; second, such a division is in accord with the basic separation between hunger and love; third, the individual carries on a "double existence" (35), by which Freud means we are both individual entities, conscious of ourselves as such, and vehicles for the indifferent reproductive capabilities of our germ plasm. Finally, Freud reminds us of one of his central beliefs, namely, that a physiological substructure will one day provide an explanation for sexuality as well as for the relationship between individual and species. "We take this probability into account when we substitute special forces in the mind for special chemical substances" (36).

Once again we encounter the difficulty of reconciling various types of discourse, various symbolic stances toward the subject of investigation. Freud admits that he is writing a metaphorical and provisional account of the psychic operations of the mind; the true account, to be written by neurophysiologists, lies in the future. Metaphorical language, a poor and temporary substitute, will one day be replaced by a univocal, quantitative, and absolutely accurate language. In the meantime, he does what he can with the limited assemblage of words, mental operations, and scientific data at his command.

But Freud continues to press the point about the physiological substratum, claiming that in the final analysis the division between ego instincts and sexual instincts rests upon a biological foundation. In concession to Jung's perspective, he admits that "when we penetrate deepest and furthest" (36), we might discover an undifferentiated energy of the mind, but such a discovery would hardly interest him, since it would not have any practical analytic significance.

To dispute or to affirm such a theory of the mind, void of any real content or utility, is equally useless (though in the essay Freud is expending a great deal of thought on just this disputation). Indeed, he asserts that such a theory of "primordial identity has as little to do with our analytical interests as the primordial kinship of all human races has to do with the proof of kinship with a testator required by the Probate Court" (36).

Perhaps there is more in such a relationship than Freud here admits, but nonetheless, he clearly champions the observable differences over the "merely theoretical" primordial identity to which Jung has pointed. An old, old battle—the Two against the One—is here being waged. Freud himself, in *Beyond the Pleasure Principle,* admits this: "Our views have from the very first been *dualistic,* and today they are even more definitely dualistic than before—now that we describe the opposition as being, not between ego-instincts and sexual-instincts but between life instincts and death instincts" (47).[6] But to maintain his dualistic perspective, Freud finds it necessary to move from a division between object and ego to the larger, even mythic, division of Eros and Thanatos.

A swarm of issues battle with one another within the text of "On Narcissism." In the section that we have been examining, there is a discursive polyphony aimed at both the clinical clarification of narcissism and at the defense of Freud's libido theory in the face of the threat from Jung's theory of "uniform mental energy." In the second section of the essay, Freud renews his analytical investigation of the phenomenon of narcissism and develops his presentation of the choice of object(s) for our love. He reiterates that schizophrenics and paranoiacs provide substantial insight into narcissism and adds that we can also study organic disease, hypochondria, and love between the sexes in order to gain clarity about the phenomenon. (Again, note how Freud casts about for evidence of narcissism, a state of being that seems to become an aspect of all human beings, not just paraphrenics.)

Although this is a wide range of conditions to investigate, his principle focus in each case is the manner in which the libido is distributed. Most importantly, every time that the libido is decathected, the person stops loving and falls ill. There is a curious circularity here: illness causes the inability to love; the inability to love causes the illness. Such a paralysis is another way of describing Narcissus as he attempts to be both the subject and object of love, a desire that engenders only despair, a sickness unto death.

The question that had bothered Freud earlier emerges once again: Why, he repeats, does the mental apparatus, which "above all [is] a device for mastering excitations" (42), tend to pass beyond narcissism to object choice? Freud's response, straight from the *Project for a Scien-*

6. This follows one page after Freud has compared those who have struggled with a definition of the instincts with the Greek natural philosophers. What are the relationships among the four elements; why does the One give way to the Many? In a certain psychological manner, Jung and Freud recapitulate the struggle among the pre-Socratics. The prize of this *agōn,* for much of contemporary critical discourse, is that Freud is taken up into the conversation about difference, while Jung, often situated as the heretical opponent, is cast into the metaphysical slough of identity. Narcissus is very much wrapped up in this *agōn.*

tific Psychology, is that "dammed-up" libido causes pain, and that pain must be relieved by a redistribution of the sexualized energy. Love is an overflow of energy that connects itself to an object that may be internal or external: ego-oriented, fantasy-oriented, or object-oriented.

Freud then turns to the "working-over"—by conversion, reaction-formation, phobias—of libidinized objects that is characteristic of schizophrenics and paranoiacs. In these people, "the libido that is liberated by frustration does not remain attached to objects in phantasy, but returns to the ego; the megalomania then represents the mastery of this volume of libido, and thus corresponds with the introversion on to the phantasy-creations that is found in the transference neuroses" (43). The "striking phenomena" of the disease—presumably the florid and systematic delusions associated with schizophrenia—are actually, for Freud, efforts at recovery; that is, the libido is once again attached to objects instead of solely to the ego.

A fundamental question arises at this juncture: How, if there is a "moment" during which the libido is attached neither to an external object nor to an internal fantasy object, could there possibly be a representation of that moment? Without at least minimal differentiation between the aspects of the psyche, there would be no "space" for reflectivity at all, no mirror for the mind's representations of itself or the other, and thus an absolute lack of self-identity.

If we shift, temporarily, from the experience of schizophrenia to that of the construction of the self, then this is perhaps the moment of scarring, the opening of the gap (Lacan's *béance*) in which mirroring of the other and thus self-identity occurs. The libido momentarily "floats" before it is organized into rudimentary I and not-I patterns. The I emerges from this emptiness and learns to speak—to be heard—within the symbolic, the dimension of signs in which we work our way back toward the origin of the self through the inevitably futile efforts of myth, literature, philosophy, and psychoanalysis.

In his discussion of schizophrenia, Freud claims that primary narcissism and megalomania eventually give way to love and the attachment to figures outside the ego. The One yields to the Many. The inchoate self is liberated from the prison that is itself, and is enabled to form bonds with the other. Moving from schizophrenia to the variations of love relationships between people, Freud distinguishes between two types of object relations: the anaclitic and the narcissistic. In the former, the "sexual instincts are at the outset supported upon the ego-instincts [the instincts of self-preservation]" (44); the earliest object of longing is the mother. In the latter situation, however, the person takes himself, or herself, as the object of love instead of the mother. "This observation," he writes, "provides us with our strongest motive for regarding the hypothesis of narcissism as a necessary one" (45).

Narcissism, then, is initially associated for Freud with the abnormal, with those whose "libidinal development has suffered some disturbance" (45), but he quickly clarifies his position, declaring that we *all* have both anaclitic and narcissistic tendencies, one of which will predominate in determining our object choices. We are all, in other words, abnormal—we are all wounded in the development of our capacities to love—and we have all moved from a stage of "primary narcissism" to more or less successful attempts to be with others in the world. This occurs before an ego has been fully constructed from the primary processes, but nonetheless, momentous choices are made. We are, as it were, there and not there when these choices are made. We must—through literature, psychoanalysis, or some other method of anamnesis—return there, to the *anderer Schauplatz* of the unconscious, if we are to undo or even recognize the effects of the first scar.

After discussing the fact that men tend to be anaclitic while women tend to be narcissistic—and then, as he did with the notion of perversity, qualifying his statement—Freud diagrams the paths leading to various object choices. A person may love:

1. According to the narcissistic type:
     a. What he is himself (actually himself)
     b. What he once was
     c. What he would like to be
     d. Someone who was once part of himself
2. According to the anaclitic type:
     a. The woman who tends
     b. The man who protects

Unable to point at a directly observable stage of primary narcissism, Freud asserts that the behavior of "fond parents" is confirmation of his theory. Their relation to "His Majesty the Baby" is characterized by "over-estimation, that sure indication of a narcissistic feature in object-choice" (48), and reveals the return of the abandoned narcissism of the parents' own infancy.

This argument, depending as it does on cultural norms—there are many situations in which children are undervalued—is not particularly convincing, but it does clearly reveal the inevitability, for psychoanalytic thinking, of the use of indirect evidence and inference about early psy-

chic conditions. It also indicates the necessarily hermeneutical manner
in which scenarios of significance are constructed from an adult, ego-
oriented perspective.

Freud, in the final section of the essay, moves directly from a discussion of narcissism in "His Majesty" to a discussion of the castration
complex, which, of course, involves another form of sceptered kingship
and serves in this context only as a brief example of the "disturbances to
which the original narcissism of the child is exposed" (49). In this final
section, Freud, assuming the psychoanalytic equivalent to physics' law of
the conservation of energy, is concerned to show what happens to the
ego libido of infantile narcissism as we grow into adults. It is not, in most
cases, clearly visible, but remains hidden. Where?

In order to answer this question, Freud turns to the psychology of
repression and discusses the ways in which a sense of being watched
develops into a conscience and an ego ideal. "Repression," Freud writes,
"proceeds from the ego; we might say with greater precision: from the
self-respect of the ego" (50). Once an ideal is formed, the ego, measuring
itself by this ideal and failing to measure up to its standards, addresses its
infantile self-love toward the ideal rather than back toward itself. The
ideal, which "deems itself the possessor of all perfections" (51), is a
substitutive form of gratification that replaces the lost narcissism of
childhood. It is, in a brilliant phrase, a "hiding place" of the libido.

The mental agency that ensures that we receive gratification from the
ego ideal, that "keeps guard" over that ideal, is the conscience, an inter-
nalization of parental and societal criticism that was "conveyed by the
medium of the voice" (53). When, in the case of paranoia and schizophrenia, the libido is withdrawn from external objects and a regression
occurs, these voices become more prominent, and the conscience—a
cacophony of voices condensed into a single authoritative monotone
against which the person is in violent rebellion—takes the form of a
"hostile influence from without" (53).

The regression toward an original narcissism, never finally attainable
except, perhaps, by the total extermination of the ego, entails an assault
on the conscience and the ego ideal guarded by the conscience, with a
subsequent "undoing" of the condensation that formed the conscience.
In a kind of psychic expansion, the voices are split apart and projected
outward to become the accusatory Furies of the paranoiac and the
schizophrenic. All this is possible, Freud suggests, because "at bottom
the self-criticism of conscience is identical with, and based upon, self-
observation" (53). The "critically watching faculty," then, becomes the

basis of conscience (as well as of those speculative, perhaps paranoiac, systems called philosophy).

From his examination of the self-regarding faculty in psychotics, Freud discusses the relationship between love and narcissism in the normal person and the neurotic (a difference of degree, not kind). The goal of a narcissistic object choice—that is, oneself, what one once was, what one would like to be, or someone who was once part of oneself—is simply to be loved. Not being loved lowers self-regard and gives rise to feelings of inferiority. "The main source of these feelings," Freud remarks, "is the impoverishment of the ego due to withdrawal from it of extraordinarily large libidinal cathexes—due, that is to say, to the injury sustained by the ego through the sexual trends which are no longer subject to control" (56). Any form of love, in other words, entails a wound.

Freud seems to be giving us no way out of the dilemma posed by narcissism, an inability to love, and the depletion of self-esteem inherent in loving another. But this is not quite the case, for he can still speak of "ego-syntonic erotic cathexes" and even of an "actual happy love." In the former, love becomes simply another activity within the dispensation of the ego; the latter, Freud appears to be claiming, occurs when the libido is returned from an object to the ego, which reconstitutes a kind of primary narcissism in which "object-libido and ego-libido cannot be distinguished" (57).

This is a very strange statement. How could such a narcissistic love possibly be restored in an adult life? On the one hand, this possibility prefigures Freud's use of the "Nirvana principle" and the "death instincts" in *Beyond the Pleasure Principle;* but, on the other, he comments that the ego is enriched by "gratification of its object-love and by fulfilling its ideals" (57). The ideal has become a substitutive object of libidinal release.

Love, in Freud's usage, is an overflow of ego libido onto an object and has the power "to remove repressions and to restore perversions" (58). Having exhausted himself by large expenditures of libido, the neurotic seeks to restore self-regard by choosing a narcissistic sexual ideal, a projected disguise of the self, rather than a "true" other. He seeks a "cure by love" rather than a cure by analysis, but "extensive repressions" usually stand in the way of the hoped-for relief from suffering.

"On Narcissism" concludes with a comment on how the wounding of the ego often leads to paranoia and the "demolition of sublimations and possible transformation of ideals in paraphrenic disorders" (59). Wounds and demolitions, pain and the recourse to a violence that is directed

either against one's self or another—these, for Freud, seem to be inherent in all of our attempts to love, to move beyond the gravitational
entrapment of the ego and out toward the other. But unless we break out
of the magic circle of the ego, unless the self-reflecting mirror of Narcissus is somehow shattered—by, for instance, a novelist or a psychoanalyst
who takes us into another register of experience—there is no hope that
the wound may be healed. And even if it is healed, the scar that marks
the place of struggle will always remain.

3

The Mirage of Narcissus:
Jacques Lacan and the Poetics
of the Psyche

I am not a poet, but a poem. A poem that is being written,
even if it looks like a subject.

—Jacques Lacan

When we move from Freud to the work of Jacques Lacan, the narcissistic scar left by the developmental vicissitudes of the ego enters the symbolic register of experience and is transformed into a text: "a page of shame that is forgotten or undone, or a page of glory that compels" (E, 52). The psychic body, from Lacan's perspective, is a text inscribed by the history of events in the unconscious; it is a readable text accessible to interpretation by the discerning eye, or the attuned ear, of the analyst. But far from being invisible or hidden away in a psychic grotto where "latent" and "real" thought exist, the unconscious lies on the surface of behavior and speech, waiting to be read, waiting to be transformed by the reading that recognizes, in all of its poignancy, the signifying letter of shame or glory.

If Freud began the psychoanalytic interpretation of narcissism, Lacan most radically furthered the work of a psychoanalytic poetics that explores the relationship between textuality, fiction, and subjectivity. And the figure of Narcissus permeates the Lacanian theory of subjectivity. I have already alluded to Lacan's statement about the "monumental construct of narcissism" that the analysand brings to the analytic session, and concerning the analytic task itself, Lacan comments that "the art of the analyst must be to suspend the subject's certainties until their last mirages have been consumed" (E, 43). We all exist in a hall of mirrors until something, some form of a true word that is based on the nothing, provides a glimpse—always surprising and unexpected, often arduously attained—beyond the wooden shed that supports the mirrors hanging on the wall. And even then, there is only a glimpse. Every subject, since every ego has been formed in the imaginary and has suffered its entry into the symbolic, is a narcissist; the illusions of narcissistic fictions are at the core of subjectivity.

Subjectivity itself—a salubrious but epiphenomenal effect of the juxtaposition of light, the psychic landscape of the other, and an angle of vision—is, for Lacan, the primary mirage. Move closer or farther away, adjust the angle of the reflective psychic apparatus, and the unified self of Descartes's *cogito* disappears without a trace. Lacan moves in very close indeed, to the point from which, as he attempts to demonstrate, the mirage shimmeringly emanates.

Psychoanalysis consumes the mirage because it alters the angle of the analysand's sight, thus enabling a different speech and a different point of view. Narcissus, as substance, or *res extensa*, does not "really" exist; he is only an optical illusion of a culture that privileges the self in order to turn away from death or its analytic equivalent, castration (which is also the beginning of symbolization). Lacan speaks to all of these issues, and I will enter his textual looking-glass with an analysis of one of his best-known essays, "The Mirror Stage as Formative of the Function of the I as Revealed in Psychoanalytic Experience," which was delivered in 1949 in Zurich.[1] After discussing this essay in some detail and refining the understanding of narcissism by glancing at material from Lacan's first seminar, I will then more explicitly address the ways in which Lacan's psychoanalytic poetics illuminate the fictionality of the subject as well as the subject of fiction.

The mirror stage is a phase of psychological development during which the preverbal infant responds to the image of the other—usually the mother's face, though the "mirror" is sometimes literal—in order to experience a unified image of his or her body and thus lay the foundation for the experience of a unified self. But as Lacan says at the beginning of the essay, "It is an experience that leads us to oppose any philosophy directly issuing from the *Cogito*" (E, 1), that is, any experience of the self that is consciously transparent to itself. Descartes's dictum is a

---

1. For a description of the history of this essay on the mirror stage, and of the difficulties in determining a beginning in such a case, see Jane Gallop's *Reading Lacan.*

leitmotiv of Lacan's thinking, and he returns time and again to it in order to modify it from a psychoanalytic point of view, with its insistence on the letter of the signifier in the unconscious.

Before the mirror, then, the child sees itself as a reflected "whole" for the first time, and "this jubilant assumption of his specular image by the child," Lacan continues, "would seem to exhibit in an exemplary situation the symbolic matrix in which the *I* is precipitated in a primordial form, before it is objectified in the dialectic of identification with the other, and before language restores it, in the universal, its function as subject" (E, 2). The I is at first a *specular image*, a mirage not yet bound to the "objectifications" of the social network or to subjectivity, which is only conferred with the advent of language use.

It is the reflective gesture of the mother, as mirror and as the symbolic matter and matrix, that grants the *infans* an illusion of wholeness and bodily integrity, which soon becomes the illusion of psychic wholeness and integrity. The infant sees the mother as a whole, then proceeds to take on her image as the image of itself. The incipient ego is the image of the other, and this "alien image" remains at the heart of selfhood as the specular ego—what Lacan also calls the "counterpart"—or the narcissistic *moi.*

The "I am who I am," in the "normal" course of things, becomes a simple assumption of identity rather than the radical question that it always, in truth, remains. Lacan's analysis, however, burns through the mirage formed by the defensively constructed "I am I" in order to demonstrate that "I am the discourse and desire of the other." Because there is no I without the other, I am inevitably and always alienated from myself, reliant upon the other to tell me who I am. In Lacan's terms, the *moi* (the narcissistic and generally unconscious subject of identifications) and the *je* (the speaking subject) are discordant just because they are able to interact, necessarily in an alienated fashion, and thereby to function as a subject that is always a divided subject.

The subject for Lacan is a function rather than a Platonic Form, an Aristotelian substance, or a Cartesian "thinking thing." Fredric Jameson comments that "psychic or affective depth is for Lacan . . . not located in the subject's relation to his own inner depths (to his own unconscious or past or whatever), but, rather in his projective relationship to that Other implied by the linguistic circuit, and only then to himself, as to an alter-ego or mirror image" (138). The *infans* becomes a subject by becoming ensnared in the nets of language and culture, an entrapment that both empowers and debilitates.

The illusory *Gestalt* of the "total form of the body" serves, Lacan

explains, "to symbolize the mental permanence of the I, at the same time
as it prefigures its alienating destination; it is still pregnant with the
correspondences that unite the I with the statue in which man projects
himself, with the phantoms that dominate him, or with the automaton in
which, in an ambiguous relation, the world of his own making tends to
find completion" (E, 3). The ego at this stage—although a "stage" is also
a repeated event or *ein anderer Schauplatz* upon which there is always
a performance occurring—is a specular ego that exists in the register of
the imaginary. It is an imago, a term introduced by Jung to refer to
autonomous and unconscious representations, a term that LaPlanche
and Pontalis define as an "unconscious prototypical figure which orien-
tates the subject's way of apprehending others" (211).[2] But what about
the ego's relation to the statue, to phantoms, and to the automaton of
which Lacan speaks so eloquently?

The statue, in which living flesh is petrified and entombed in stone,[3] is
the result of the necessary objectification of the specular ego. As Lacan
puts it in another essay, it is the subject's "capture in an objectification—
no less imaginary than before—of his static state or of his 'statue': in a
renewed status of his alienation" (E, 43). The statue is the mistaken
assumption that the "I" that speaks is the same as the "me" that is spoken
of. Insofar as self-knowledge entails the project of making ourselves an
object of thought, we remain alienated from ourselves. How else might
self-knowledge be imagined?

The statue is the frozen self, aligned by Lacan with death and the
unspeakable; it is the self that analysis, as well as efficacious reading and
writing, breathes into in order to revive the renounced being of flesh
and blood, a being that can speak freely of—about and from—itself. A
hardened mirage, to use an awkward and stiff figure of speech, the statue
believes itself impermeable to change and shows a face of stone to the
world. The statue is the symbol of the "mental permanence of the I" in
which each of us projects him- or herself into the world, in which we
don masks and personify ourselves, usually forgetting that we are players
on a stage. The statue is the persona. It is a mummy rather than a

---

2. In *Symbols of Transformation* (44n), Jung discusses his use of the imago. He relates it
to the complex and the archetype, as well as to the Schreber case and to Carl Spitteler's novel
Imago (Jena, 1919). For Jung, of course, all of these terms, especially "archetype," have an
emphatically collective dimension. Work remains to be done situating Jung's "collective unconscious" in relation to Lacan's symbolic dimension.

3. Mark Taylor, in his chapter on Lacan in *Altarity,* discusses the relationship of Medusa to
Lacan's thought.

mummer, and the difference between these two is at the heart of any possible transformation of Narcissus.

Close by the nocturnal statue lurk phantoms that, as Lacan contends, dominate us. The phantoms are the elusive imagos of others in which we have our being; they are the unconscious fantasies that structure our being-in-the-world; they are what I will call, in my discussion of *Daniel Martin,* the "ghosts in the greenwood," repressed figures that must be recovered through the act of writing before narcissism can be overcome. The phantoms, too, are all the objects of desire that can never become possessions, longings that can never be fulfilled. The phantoms beckon and drive, pursue and attract, but can never be possessed.

The automaton is that "in which, in an ambiguous relation, the world of his [man's] own making tends to find completion" (3). With the automaton, derived from Aristotle's *Physics* IV–V, Lacan gestures toward the fact that we are all bound by the repetition compulsion, which, in its turn, emerges from the death instinct explored first by Freud in *Beyond the Pleasure Principle.* Not only do we find literal "completion" in the return to death, but all of our significations rest upon the ceaselessly moving chain of signifiers, which, acting like an automaton, is itself founded on the death of presence (of the mother, the first love object, etc.).

Our relation to language is ambiguous because it kills us in order that we may live; only in the alienating ambience of the symbolic—the linguistic and cultural realm—can we become subjects; but as subjects severed by the signifier, we are necessarily cut off from the real, which "is beyond the *automaton,* the return, the coming-back, the insistence of the signs by which we see ourselves governed by the pleasure principle" (Lacan, *Four Fundamental Concepts,* 54; hereafter cited as FFC).

Speaking in the "Agency of the Letter in the Unconscious" about the indestructibility of unconscious desire, Lacan notes that "it is in a memory, comparable to what is called by that name in our modern thinking-machines (which are in turn based on an electronic realization of the composition of signification), it is in this sort of memory that is found the chain that *insists* on reproducing itself in the transference, and which is the chain of dead desire" (E, 167). The process of making meaning brings death, and life with it, in the form of a sign. When the sign becomes a symptom, it is an indication that in the patient's history desire has somewhere died. All this will automatically reappear in the transference. The automaton, therefore, is the symptom of unlived history; it is the scar that appears time and time again among the phantoms, of which "we" are one.

Narcissus, then, can be understood under the sign of any of the three figures: statue, phantom, or automaton. He is a statue because he has hardened himself to the yearning entreaties of those beautiful young men and women and of the nymphs who plead for his attention. In seeing only himself, he becomes his own Medusa, turns himself to stone, and sinks into the waters toward Hades. Or, in a more prosaic style, the statuesque quality of narcissism connotes the "formal stagnation or fixa-tion of feelings and images, which constitute the subject and its objects (others) with attributes of permanence, identity, and substantiality" (Ragland-Sullivan, *Jacques Lacan,* 43; hereafter cited as JL).

As a phantom, Narcissus tries to be the object of his own fantasy, to become his own foundational imago. The reflection in the pool is unreal, without substance—because without genuine otherness. Narcis-sus, driven by the fantasy, plunges toward the fantasy to his death. In less metaphorical terms, the narcissist organizes existence as an at-tempt to return to the original narcissistic moment of the mother-child dyad at the instant of mirroring. Such a movement is tantamount to death, for at that monistic moment there was no subject.

There, in that union not known as union, before the cut of the law, was *jouissance;* there the I longs to be and therefore compulsively thrusts against the door that bars the way back and that also separates the signifier from the signified. But the subject thrusts against a nothing, against a mirage that dissolves like air, like the cool waters of a pond held in cupped hands. Narcissistic satisfaction cannot be reclaimed; the mother is gone, and we are left with silly games with spinning spools. We cannot have the fullness of desire, which was before—and may be after—the time of subjectivity, but we can play with words. We can read and write.

As automaton, Narcissus repeats his frustrated desire for the phantom object until death puts an end to that desire. He intones a silent "I" as he stretches out over the smooth pool. The "I" that becomes "Eye"—an ancient conjunction in Western metaphysics—seeks its satisfaction in a vision of the "same," wanting simultaneously to see and be seen, to be the voyeur and the exhibitionist. The Eye wants to be the I of God and sweep up everything within its omnipotent gaze.[4]

But we are not yet through with Lacan's essay on the mirror stage, and

---

4.   Lacan makes a great deal out of the difference between the "Eye" and the "Gaze." (See, for instance, *The Four Fundamental Concepts of Psycho Analysis.*)

I want to return to the formation of the I. "The important point," Lacan writes, "is that this form [the primordial form of the ideal I] situates the agency of the ego, before its social determination, in a *fictional direction* which will always remain irreducible for the individual alone, or rather, which will only rejoin the coming-into-being of the subject asymptotically, whatever the success of the dialectical syntheses by which he must resolve as 'I' his discordance with his own reality" (E, 2; emphasis added).

Lacan is speaking of the I before its entry into the symbolic sphere of language and culture, just before it leaves the imaginary of the mirror experience for the discordance brought on by the cut of castration and the Law of the Father. And, already and forever after, the ego is situated as a fiction that will never, given the nature of desire, be able to rejoin the real to create a perfectly harmonious, unified, or total, self. Such a harmonizing of the *moi* (the original specular ego in the "mirror") and the *je* (the speaking self of the postimaginary stages) can at best only occur "asymptotically," approaching nearer and nearer to each other but never meeting (a union that would be Sartre's in-itself-for-itself, or God).

The moment at which the mirror stage ends "decisively tips the whole of human knowledge into mediatization through the desire of the other, constitutes its objects in an abstract equivalence by the co-operation of others, and turns the I into that apparatus for which every instinctual thrust constitutes a danger" (E, 5). The self is made up of, patched together by perceptions of, the desire of the other; the self is a myth, a fine example of Lévi-Strauss's bricolage.

Far from being an autonomous entity—which itself is part of the fantasy of narcissism—the ego is built up by a process of what Lacan calls *méconnaissance:* misconstructions, misconstruals, and the illusions objectified as statue and phantom. The ego, in other words, is a layered text of fictions, pages wet and torn, the ink running, cut and pasted pages of shame and glory. And every reading, or attempt at reading, produces new pages.

Lacan concludes his 1949 essay by declaring that "in the recourse of subject to subject that we preserve, psychoanalysis may accompany the patient to the ecstatic limit of the *Thou art that,* in which is revealed to him the cipher of his mortal destiny, but it is not in our mere power as practitioners to bring him to that point where the real journey begins" (E, 7). Psychoanalysis, even the structuralist analysis that emphasizes the construction of the subject by the symbolic networks in which the subject comes into being, preserves the relationship of subject to subject (rather than subject to its own ego, though that, too, is involved).

In fact, it is only because of this preservation, from Lacan's viewpoint, that the "true word," which requires a listener, can be spoken. This speech fulfills the intent of psychoanalysis, which "can have for its goal only the advent of a true speech and the realization by the subject of his history in his relation to a future" (E, 88). At the completion of the cure effected by intersubjective speech, the analysand recognizes that "this being has never been anything more than his construct in the imaginary and that this construct disappoints all his certainties.... For in this la- bour which he undertakes to reconstruct *for* another, he rediscovers the fundamental alienation that made him construct it *like another,* and which has always destined it to be taken from him *by another*" (E, 42). Living in a mirage of self-direction and autonomy, the narcissist forgets the other—as the object of desire and as the object of identification by which one structures one's subjectivity—and can thus never speak truly.

The capacity for true speech, which is closer to Nietzsche's *amor fati* and Heidegger's being-toward-death than to any theory of truth based on correlation between word and factual reality, is still on "this side" of the "real journey" Lacan mentions—although, since the future of the authen- tic cannot be predicted, he leaves the phrase without a specific referent. But psychoanalysis is nonetheless able to bring the subject close to the "ecstatic limit of the *Thou art that,*" an experience that however much it resembles the initial narcissistic identification with the primary other in which I believe myself to be you—I see myself in the mirror of you—is nonetheless on the other side of the disillusioning dissolution of the mirages of narcissism effected by the analytic work.

"Thou art that" is the absolute metaphor, and absolute metaphor de- stroys metaphor and therefore speech itself. Absolute metaphor: meta- phor extended so far that the tension between likeness and difference snaps, and the subject vanishes altogether. Subjectivity is constituted by the action of metaphor, by the capacity to say, "I am like and not like."[5] (We will soon see the various ways in which Abel Tiffauges and Daniel Martin are, respectively, subsumed by and craft the action of metaphor.)

When psychoanalysis and reading and writing extend into the *Tat Tvam Asi,* they surpass their limits and destroy themselves. If we are to speak of subjectivity as a text and the texts of the subject, if we are to learn about narcissism from reading and writing, we cannot leave the

5.   This capacity is linked by Fredric Jameson to Hegel and, especially, to Sartre's distinc- tion between internal and external negations. Jameson states that "human reality is governed by the internal negation; so that the fact that I am not an engineer, or a Chinese, or a sixty-year-old, says something that touches me profoundly in my very being. So [too] with language" (34).

symbolic, with its inscription of mortality and history, behind in order to step beyond the ecstatic limit. We must, for the time of thinking, remain within Lacan's Borromean knot of the imaginary, the symbolic, and the real.

Having presented Lacan's essay on the mirror stage, I now want to turn to Lacan's first *Seminar* (hereafter cited as S), in order to clarify his understanding of narcissism, a task that requires a deeper understanding of the imaginary and its relation to the subject. In section 7, "The Topic of the Imaginary," Lacan recounts the "experiment of the inverted bouquet" as a metaphor that will "illustrate in a particularly simple way what follows on from the strict intrication of the imaginary world and the real world in the psychic economy" (S, 78).[6] He has already contextualized his remarks by mentioning the seventh chapter of the *Interpretation of Dreams,* in which Freud leaves anatomy behind for the psychic dimension of the mental apparatus, and by reminding his reader that psychic reality stands between perception and the "motor consciousness of the ego" (S, 75). The psyche has its own way of being, its own phenomenology, and it is this realm of meaning and the loss of meaning, not neurology or behaviorism, that is the proper domain of psychoanalysis.

Rather than repeating the structure of the experiment, let me simply cite Lacan's conclusions about it:

> For there to be an illusion, for there to be a world constituted, in front of the eye looking, in which the imaginary can include the real and, by the same token, fashion it, in which the real also can include and, by the same token, locate the imaginary, one condition must be fulfilled—as I have said, the eye must be in a specific position, it must be inside the cone. If it is outside the cone, it will no longer see what is imaginary, for the simple reason that nothing from the cone of emission will happen to strike it. It will see things in their real state, entirely naked, that is to say, inside the mechanism, a sad, empty pot, or some lonesome flowers, depending on the case. (S, 80)

The imaginary includes and shapes the real, and the real includes and locates the imaginary. It is this conjunction that allows illusion, a microcosm of the human experience of the world, to occur. The world, represented here by an image created by the experimental structure, is real

6. My dictionary defines "intrication" as "entanglement," and notes that it is obsolete. Reading Lacan will teach one more than French.

and unreal; it is the given and the constructed; it is, in a word, the *fictional.* By implication, the real, of itself, does not constitute a world, at least not for mortals. As Lacan remarks, "The gods belong to the field of the real" (FFC, 45), but humans are knots and Möbius strips.

True, one can with such experiments at any time step outside of the "cone of emission" and annihilate the little image; one can stand to one side and see the "naked" reality, the empty pot and the lonesome flowers that are brought together only as a mirage when the eye is positioned within the cone where the rays of light will intersect. One can without trouble step outside of the field of Narcissus, a mere character in an antiquated poem, and instantaneously see things quite differently. But every shift of point of view involves a loss as well as a gain.

Lacan writes that "in the relation to the imaginary and the real, and in the constitution of the world such as results from it, everything depends on the position of the subject. And the position of the subject ... is essentially characterised by its place in the symbolic world, in other words in the world of speech" (S, 80). What is Narcissus's place in the symbolic; what is his type of speech?

In section 9, "On Narcissism," Lacan begins to answer this question. "Speech," he argues, "can express the being of the subject, but, up to a certain point, it never succeeds in so doing" (S, 107). For the most part, that is, the analysand engages in a form of "empty speech," a form of talking reminiscent of Heidegger's "idle chatter of the They" but complicated by the split within the subject between the *moi* and the *je,* as well as the split between subject and subject.

When analysis cures, "full" speech takes the place, though this is not a conclusive triumph, of its false twin. Curative speech is speech which "aims at, which forms, the truth such as it becomes established in the recognition of one person by another. Full speech is speech which performs. One of the subjects finds himself, afterwards, other than he was before" (S, 107). The goal of psychoanalysis is a transformation of the subject through the means of the spoken word, a goal that in my view is rigorously analogous to the goal of literature in the medium of written texts. And, as Lacan observes, this is a conjoint *formation* of the truth, not a discovery of an already established truth. Full speech is speech that makes not simply a play of signifiers, though it is that as well, but a place for truth between people. It is, in other words, a form of poiesis.

Lacan then discusses Freud's "On Narcissism" and, especially, why Freud worked so diligently to contest Jung's perspective on the unitary character of the libido. Freud's wish is to defend a dualistic conception of the libido that maintains the distinctions between egoistic and sexual energy, but, as Lacan asks, "How can these terms be clearly distinguished if one maintains the idea that they are equivalent in energetic terms, which is what allows one to say that it is in so far as the libido is disinvested from the object that it returns back on to the ego?" (S, 115). Lacan argues that this difficulty is why Freud conceived narcissism as a "secondary" process, for a "unity comparable to the ego does not exist at the beginning, *nicht von Anfang,* is not to be found in the individual from the start, and the *Ich* has to develop, *entwickelt werden.* The auto-erotic instincts, in contrast, are there right from the start" (S, 115). Autoerotism, then, would be the equivalent to "primary" narcissism, a reservoir of energy not yet pseudopodically cathected onto objects in the world.

Lacan proceeds to connect this moment with his own conception of the mirror stage:

> The *Urbild,* which is a unity comparable to the ego, is constituted at a specific moment in the history of the subject, at which point the ego begins to take on its functions. This means that the human ego is founded on the basis of the imaginary relation. The func-tion of the ego, Freud writes, must have *eine neue psychische Aktion . . . zu gestalten.* In the development of the psyche, some-thing new appears whose function is to give form to narcissism. (S, 115)

Primary narcissism, which occurs at the nondifferentiated level of autoerotic instincts, is modified when "something new" appears, and out of the basically unformed instincts comes a cosmos of the psyche; the *Urbild* of the mirror stage gives rise to the ego. The specular ego gives way to the social ego at the threshold experience Eco calls a "structural crossroads" (203).

The "form" of narcissism, the ego of the symbolic stage, is founded upon the mirage of the image, the "subject's relation to its formative identifications" (S, 116) within the imaginary. The ego itself is the "monu-mental construct of narcissism," and it is this statuesque ego that is deconstructed, and thereby remade, in the speech between analyst and analysand. So, too, with the deconstruction of relatively stable texts. The meanings of a text, once they have been remorselessly taken apart oppo-sition by opposition, will not lie idly about on the critic's shelf but will immediately knit into a new text that echoes the old.

Lacan's discussion of the ego and the imaginary leads him to explicate the meaning of Freud's statement that the schizophrenic, unlike the neurotic, "seems really to have withdrawn his libido from persons and things in the outer world, without replacing them by others in his phantasy" (N, 31). The neurotic retains his relation to the real, however distorted such a relation might be, through his or her fantasies. The psychotic is barred from fantasy and therefore from the real.

Psychosis therefore, for Lacan, does not occur within the imaginary but is a twist of the symbolic, the dimension that deals specifically with language. As he comments, "We will see that it may be the case that the specific structure of the psychotic should be located in a symbolic unreal, or in a symbolic unmarked by the unreal. The function of the imaginary is to be located somewhere entirely different" (S, 117). In an essay in which he explores Schreber's paranoid delusions,[7] Lacan remarks, "We will take *Verwerfung,* then, to be a *foreclosure* of the signifier. To the point at which the Name-of-the-Father is called . . . may correspond in the Other, then, a mere hole, which, by the inadequacy of the metaphoric effect will provoke a corresponding hole at the place of the phallic signification" (E, 201). This, then, is the principle distinction between psychosis and neurosis—the former withdraws libido from external objects without a substitute—with which Freud was concerned in the above-cited passage of "On Narcissism."

Laplanche and Pontalis clarify this *Verwerfung,* this foreclosure, noting that it "consists in not symbolising what ought to be symbolised (castration): it is a 'symbolic abolition' " (168). It is a hole, a tear, in the symbolic, rather than a symbolized hole. The lack of castration and the lack of the total fulfillment of desire by the other is rejected from the structure of the subject. It therefore does not return as the repressed, which is the condition of the neurotic; it returns from the real: as paranoid delusions that, since the analytical relationship depends on the imaginary and symbolic relationship of transference, are not amenable to psychoanalysis.

I have taken this detour into the structure of psychosis because of its pertinence to the question of language and to the problem of the relationship among the "lunatic, the lover, and the poet." In a word, literature is not psychotic language, regardless of its appearance at times, because it is a unifying *agōn* of the imaginary and the symbolic that cannot return from the real as a *delusion* just because it is situated within the sphere of the recognizably illusory, within a fictional world.

7. This essay, "On a Question Preliminary to Any Possible Treatment of Psychosis," is part of a seminar that Lacan delivered in 1955–56.

An artistic work of the imagination is one in which the imaginary is formalized by the symbolic and the symbolic is dynamized by the imaginary. Such a view also suggests that the presence of fantasy and image, far from indicating an "escape" from reality, indicates that it is possible by reading and writing for one to brush up against, though never to live within, the realm of the real.

Both the artistic text and the human subject are fictions. Just as the subject is engendered by the passage through the mirror stage into the symbolic world—where the imaginary continues to be operative—so, too, the texts of fiction exist within both the imaginary and the symbolic registers. Texts, therefore, can either be interpreted by the rigorous formalisms of semiotics and linguistics or by the hermeneutics that sees private or public fantasies enacted at a more "macrocosmic" level of the text. Since the subject is like a text, the shift from the subject to the text involves not a completely new orienting philosophy or set of methodological tools but only a slight shift of focus, a readjustment of the interpretive lens.

Most significantly for the purpose of moving Lacan's thought beyond the domain of clinical psychoanalysis toward literary texts, Lacan remarks that the primordial form of the I "situates the agency of the ego, before its social determination, in a *fictional* direction which will always remain irreducible for the individual alone" (E, 2; emphasis added). The self begins as a mirage, a reflection. The question that will henceforth concern us, then, is not *whether* the self is a fiction, but *how* the self is a fiction. What are the forms of fictionality that the subject employs? And what is the relationship between the fictive self and the fictive text?

Shoshana Felman articulately demonstrates this "likeness" between subject and text, arguing that the originality, for Lacan, of Freud's discovery of the unconscious is not that it exists, but that it speaks and that it is structured like a language. "This is what constitutes the *radicality* of the Freudian unconscious, which is not simply *opposed* to consciousness, but speaks as something other *from within* the speech of consciousness, which it undercuts, subverts. The unconscious is thenceforth no longer— as it has traditionally been conceived—the simple outside of the conscious, but rather a division, *Spaltung,* cleft, *within* consciousness itself" ("Originality," 48). The subject is a Möbius strip on which consciousness and unconsciousness are always copresent.

Like consciousness and the unconscious, psychoanalysis and literature are implicated with each other, folded in around each other. This is the thrust of Felman's argument in "On Reading Poetry," in which she discusses Poe's much debated "Purloined Letter." She argues that

> psychoanalytic theory and the literary text mutually inform—and
> displace—each other; since the very position of the interpreter—
> of the analyst—turns out to be not *outside,* but *inside* the text,
> there is no longer a clear-cut opposition or a well-defined border
> between literature and psychoanalysis: psychoanalysis could be
> intraliterary just as much as literature is intrapsychoanalytic. The
> methodological stake is no longer that of the *application* of psy-
> choanalysis *to* literature, but rather, of the *interimplication in*
> each other. (145)

Conscious, unconscious; reader, text; analysand, analyst—all are inter-
woven. And, in each case, the most fascinating point at which to attempt to
position oneself—since "inside" and "outside" have begun to blur—is on
the line, a jagged line that appears and disappears, between the two terms.

As I make the transition of focus between subject and text, the most
obvious route to take would be to address once more the reading of
Poe's "Letter" through the Lacanian "letter," but I prefer to begin with
Boaz, who is a wealthy landowner in the village of Bethlehem. This is
where Lacan also begins, in "The Agency of the Letter in the Unconscious," when he discusses the place of metaphor in the "effective field
constituted by the signifier" (E, 156), the other side of which is
metonymy, the trope of contiguity and desire.

Lacan, turning to Quillet's French dictionary, chooses a line from Vic-
tor Hugo's poem "Boaz Asleep": "His sheaf was neither miserly nor spite-
ful." It is not the sheaf of wheat itself that is the true source of generosity,
but Boaz, the kinsman of Elimelech. But Boaz, as Lacan points out, is
nowhere in the line of poetic speech; we are given only the possessive
pronoun "his." Lacan's argument continues:

> But once *his* sheaf has thus usurped his place, Booz [Boaz] can no
> longer return there; the slender thread of the little word *his* that
> binds him to it is only one more obstacle to his return in that it
> links him to the notion of possession that retains him at the heart
> of greed and spite. So *his* generosity, affirmed in the passage, is yet
> reduced to *less than nothing* by the munificence of the sheaf
> which, coming from nature, knows neither our reserve nor our
> rejections, and even in its accumulation remains prodigal by our
> standards. (E, 157)

Boaz is cast out by the presence of his sheaf in a line of poetry—the
metaphorical substitute for himself as subject and subjector—and by the

sheaf's metonymical relation to nature in its prodigious prodigality in which it wanders where it will, far from where we demand its home be, giving forth without calculation.

The sheaf is not only metaphor, though that is the aspect Lacan stresses in his analysis, but also a metonymy for nature's abundance, for the wealth of Boaz and—with perhaps a slight exaggeration—for the "Book of Ruth" that is itself metonymical of the entire saga of Israel's relation with God in the Hebrew Bible. That is, in its poetic usage, "his sheaf" not only substitutes for Boaz "one word for another" (E, 157), but it also stands in a part-to-whole relationship with the other terms I have mentioned.

And although Boaz disappears in the operation of metaphor, he can reappear through the operation of a simple critical practice: recalling the story of Naomi, Ruth, and the generous kinsman who takes the foreigner into his family. Famine and death, utter lack, generate the plot of the short narrative of Ruth's return from Moab, her native country, to Bethlehem, where she meets the wealthy landowner who is the kinsman second in line for her hand in marriage. To marry Ruth, Boaz must negotiate at the city's gate with the rightful owner of the marriage rights. In order to signify consent in a relationship of "redemption and exchange," one man "drew off his sandal and gave it to the other, and this was the manner of attesting in Israel" (Ruth 4:7). Boaz and Ruth are married, and she gives birth to Obed, who fathers Jesse, and so on down the line.

Commenting on Lacan's analysis of the sheaf, Elizabeth Wright observes that "Lacan likens the pattern of metaphor to what happens when the Father's Law, the 'Name-of-the-Father,' replaces the 'Desire of the Mother.' . . . Where the Desire of the Mother was a lure, the metaphor of the Father's word becomes a kind of trick, playing with an interanimation of the old desire with a promised, forever deferred satisfaction of that desire" (112). The "trick," as Wright says, is that the sheaf, as phallic signifier, pretends to promise generosity, whereas, in fact, it is "the result of the split caused in the subject upon entry to the Symbolic" (112). Ruth and Boaz seem to have had their desire satisfied within the law of the symbolic, but as for the larger patrilinear sense of promise, I will leave that for others to debate.

At least in this example, then, Boaz can "reappear" if we have sufficient knowledge and can adequately elaborate from the condensed metaphor back to its abundant source (which, needless to say, is not history but another text). But Lacan is quite correct in stating that as soon as we explicitly move into the poetic sphere itself, Boaz as person and proper name vanishes, only to reappear as a sheaf (of grain and of paper). "But if in this profusion," Lacan writes, "the giver has disappeared along with his gift, it is only in order to rise again in what surrounds the figure of speech in which he was annihilated" (E, 157). Poetry is a resurrection of the lost father (and recall Freud's analysis of the epic poet in *Totem and Taboo*).

Absence grounds presence; the "death" of Boaz enables the life of the poetic metaphor to begin. This is the case not only with this poem but with the poetic in general, which represents the process of symbolization in its entirety. From a Lacanian point of view, subjectivity and textuality both originate in a cutting off, a giving up, and a death that grants form to the flux of the imaginary.

Lacan discusses this process at some length at the conclusion to "The Function and Field of Speech and Language in Psychoanalysis." The context of his commentary on the birth of symbolization is, in general, his discussion of the transference and the repetition compulsion and, more specifically, of Freud's grandson's game with the spinning reel: *Fort! Da!* As Lacan says, "Thus the symbol manifests itself first of all as the murder of the thing, and this death constitutes in the subject the eternalization of his desire. The first symbol in which we recognize humanity in its vestigial traces is the sepulture, and the intermediary of death can be recognized in every relation in which man comes to the life of his history" (E, 104). The moment of enunciation destroys the thing itself, whatever such an experience might have entailed, and simultaneously gives us the capacity to bear loss and to make of ourselves the speaking mediator—from a third place—of the here and the there, the present and the nonpresent.

This third place is the place of the full speech of either a subject or a text. Such speech occurs as an activity *between* two interlocutors; it is an intersubjective event that "moves towards nothing less than a transformation of the subject . . . and the realization by the subject of his history in his relation to a future" (E, 83, 88). When true speech occurs, it is always accompanied by strong affects such as love, hate, or a quiet ecstasy. And although Lacan is talking specifically about the psychoanalytic encounter, the same is true for the experience of literature.

Writing-reading is both a resistance to and a love affair with death, a stand-in for the "mother"—whether the biological mother, nature, or the gods—who has absconded. Where has she gone? We write letters— sometimes called novels and sometimes philosophy—in the hope of finding her. There will of course be no response, for she is one version of what Lacan names the "dead partner" (E, 103), which, never accessible of itself, enables symbolization to occur. But her silence in the face of our desire is not sufficient reason to stop writing.

On the contrary, the abundant poverty of writing—and this is especially true of myth and the various forms of literature—undertakes the impossible task of filling the *béance* left by her absence and thereby creates a living memorial to her.[8] Literature, to employ Lacan's terminology, could be said to be the grateful, if essentially superfluous, gesture of the Law of the Father toward the Desire of the Mother, mediatively enacted by the writing subject.

But a Lacanian poetic that joins, through a bond of metaphor, the subject and the text is not solely reliant upon the death of the thing as the beginning of the word. Literature, though dependent on the binary opposition represented by *fort-da*, is not exhausted by this formula. Ellie Ragland-Sullivan, for example, contends that literature exerts such power on the reader because "it is an allegory of the psyche's fundamental structure" ("Prolegomena," 381), and the specific mechanisms of the allegory are elucidated by her understanding of Lacan's formulations about the psyche.

Basing her suggestions upon Lacan's distinction between the *je* and the *moi*, the narcissistic "self" that "believes the myths that constitute it as a fiction" (387), she suggests that "psychoanalysis is an *Ur*-theory of which literature is an *Ur*-dramatization" (386). This is the same dual structure that orients my own thinking; psychoanalysis and literature are two forms of symbolization that rotate around the necessary condition for symbolization, the nothing: the gap, the indeterminacy of the truly fictional, the mythical origin of the ten thousand things.

Narcissus, in this context, represents more than Freud's autoerotic instincts and the return of the libido from objects, the early identificatory fictions of the Lacanian *moi*, or the self-reflexivity of modern and postmodern fiction. He also represents symbolization attempting to catch itself in its own reflection, to grasp itself in a speculative gaze. But a breeze comes up and disturbs the water; the image is gone and Narcissus is bound for Hades. The discourse of Narcissus becomes, always, a long and circuitous course into the dark world of Dis.

Having remarked that "the *moi* reveals *je* as an unreliable narrator," Ragland-Sullivan offers a basis for a broad theory of literature's efficacy from a Lacanian perspective:

---

8. I am in part thinking of Eric Gould's ideas on myth and, at a much farther remove, of Bartleby and the dead-letter box.

If the *moi* operates perception, both the author's and the reader's, through a kind of representational dispersion within language, then literary texts unveil the Real fictionality of "self." Such
a connection between language, identity and mind would go a
long way toward solving the riddle of the "truth-value" of literature. Like Lacan's vision of psychic experience, literary discourse
would operate by sliding from one perceptual register to another:
the Imaginary (identificatory fusions), the Symbolic (language,
cultural codes and conventions), the Real (what *is*), and the Symptom. . . . These four registers prescribe protean waltzes around a
void: what one knows (but misrecognizes and denies) about
one's unconscious. (387)

The subject is fictional in much the same way as a novel is fictional, and
since there is an affinity between the two, literature is able to transfigure
the self's experience of itself and its relationship to the world, including
its narcissistic fixations, defenses, and its illusions about its grandiosities.

Lacan, then, the psychoanalyst most attuned to the complexities,
obdurateness, and mysteries of language, sets the stage—as director,
prompter, actor, and stagehand—for our step into the play of fiction
itself, where Narcissus is fully metaphorized. Reading Lacan lets us hear
more fully the whisper of the sliding signifiers and the more brazen
clangs of the erotic struggle between metaphor and metonymy, between symptom and desire.

Through his practice and his speculations on the specularity of the I,
Lacan establishes that the poetic functions of signification and the figurative work of metaphor and metonymy are at the heart of subjectivity.
Whereas Narcissus believes that the poem of the self can be completed
and then mummified into the dead letter of a completely self-sufficient
interpretation, Lacan insists that the poem that we are as subjects is a
poem never completed but always in the making.

4

The Voice of Narcissus:
Identity and Nothingness in *The Waves*

The synthesis of my being: how only writing composes it; how nothing makes a whole unless I am writing.

—Virginia Woolf

The artist: melancholy's most intimate witness and the most ferocious combatant of the symbolic abdication enveloping [*her*]—until death strikes and suicide imposes its triumphant conclusion upon the void of the lost object.

—Julia Kristeva

Literature, as the formal and animated expression of the absence and presence entailed in any act of symbolization, contains death within itself. From word to word, sentence to sentence, literature veers between its speaking subject—the individual authorial voice working upon the structures of language—and the subject of which it speaks, its thematic content. The meaning of the text, like that of the self, is composed, decomposes, and is recomposed with each new reader and each new context of reading. The many voices of a text are brought into a unified voice only to be dispersed once more in the currents of language and temporality.

In *The Waves,* Virginia Woolf creates a composite self out of six separate voices, voices that speak in order to know themselves, or at least represent themselves, and as a means of resisting the inevitability of death. In the process of forming their identity, otherness—the otherness of friends, of language, of the world, and of the nothing—is brought into the center of that identity, disrupting its continuity and unity. Emile

Benveniste has argued that "it is by identifying himself as a unique person pronouncing *I* that each speaker sets himself up in turn as the 'subject' " (220), and this is a precise description of the genesis, and the erosion, of subjectivity in *The Waves.* The speaking voice, narrated as written prose, simultaneously grants and undercuts the sense of identity.

At the conclusion of the days and seasons of the novel, Bernard, a poet and the central voice of the novel, takes it upon himself to "sum up" the stories previously recited, "to explain . . . the meaning of my life" (341). He concludes by identifying with Percival and valiantly exclaiming, "Death is the enemy. It is death against whom I ride" (383). But Percival, the hero of both the Grail legends and of Woolf's sextet, died ignominiously when his horse tripped in a molehill, and Bernard's romantic bombast remains unconvincing—the desperate, mortal voice of Narcissus in the face of that which has true power rather than only a fantasied omnipotence. I will return to the conclusion of the novel, but we must first attend to the tension between recitation and self-reflection, self-reflection as recitation, and reflection and death.

The Waves is not so much the story, a developed plot that verbally mimes action in the world, of six characters named Bernard, Louis, Neville, Jinny, Rhoda, and Susan—with Percival, alive and dead, looming behind them all—as it is the discursive enactment of a single poetic voice in six closely related keys. Eric Warner has remarked that "one of the greatest peculiarities of *The Waves* is that it seems to be all on the surface; the six figures whose speech absorbs the narrative are in a sense critics themselves, perpetually engaged in an attempt to read the text of their lives, and establish the pattern, links, recurrent motifs, structures contained therein" (3). The play of language on a textual or psychic surface is something that we have come to expect from twentieth-century narratives, as is the attempt to read the "text" of existence, and the insistence on speech—on the way character is enacted as voice—brings us directly into the realm of the "talking cure," which, as Lacan insists, is the "single medium" (E, 40) of psychoanalytic work.

If among the welter of voices in *The Waves,* I am attempting to remain particularly attuned to the distinctive voice of Narcissus, what is the tone of his voice? It is a lament. As Julia Kristeva notes, the "speaking being is a wounded being, his speech wells up out of an aching for love, and the 'death drive' (Freud) or the 'unbeing' (Lacan) that are coextensive with human nature" (*Tales of Love,* 372; hereafter cited as TL). The speakers called Bernard, Louis, Neville, Jinny, Susan, and Rhoda speak out of a wounded being, and it is a speech that never quite reaches another—except insofar as that other is a reader—and always circulates back to the speaker. In her diary, Woolf declared that *The Waves* was an "abstract mystical eyeless book: a play-poem" (134). In this poetic prose, Narcissus speaks from emptiness and melancholy because he can never grasp the other, the other always just beyond the fingertips or the carrying power of the voice, and is therefore thrown back upon the nothing from which speech struggles to stand apart.

Kristeva further elaborates upon the source of the speech that constitutes an author's work:

> His sorrow would be the most archaic expression of a narcissistic wound, unable to be symbolized or named, too precocious for any exterior agent (subject or object) to be correlated to it. For this type of narcissistic depressive, sorrow is in reality his only object; more exactly, it constitutes a substitute object to which he clings, cultivating and cherishing it, for lack of any other. In this context, suicide is not a camouflaged act of war but a reuniting with sorrow and, beyond it, with that impossible love, never attained, always elsewhere; such are the promises of the void, of death. (MI, 107)

Literature, from this perspective, is the voice of sorrow that is finally nonrepresentable; literature is forever doomed to fail in its most fundamental task of the recovery of that which has been lost, of resurrecting the dead. Given what we know of Woolf's life and death, such an analysis is all the more poignant, but it is only the text of the novel, with its composition of subjectivities generated by desire and death, that will help us to think more deeply about the relationship between textuality and subjectivity, about the loneliness and depression of Narcissus as the speaking writer, and about the mirror and nothingness.

The Waves opens with a simple narration of a setting: "*The sun had not yet risen. The sea was indistinguishable from the sky except that the sea was slightly creased as if a cloth had wrinkles in it*" (179). No sooner are the encompassing images of sea and sky introduced than the work of the metaphorical "as if" begins, wrinkling the cloth of the sea and lighting the infinite fuse of signification. We read that there is a garden and a house, although within the bedroom "all was dim and unsubstantial" (180). The human world, initially asleep, is coextensive with the natural world.

Bernard's is the first voice: " 'I see a ring,' said Bernard, 'hanging above me. It quivers and hangs in a loop of light' " (180).[1] Or is it the first? Before Bernard speaks, there is already, and this is always the case for any speaker, the presence of the world in which he speaks. This is enacted not only by the third person narrative of the "introduction" to each of the nine sections of the novel but, in Bernard's opening lines, by the intertextual resonance with Henry Vaughan's vision in "The World": "I saw eternity the other night / Like a great ring of pure and endless light." And then there is the disturbingly simple phrase that recurs like an automaton marking the space of speech throughout the novel, "Bernard said."

We know, of course, that it is Woolf arranging her text as she goes, setting her speakers forth and apart from one another, but to what does this simple observation point? In part, it means that since Bernard's voice is embedded within the narrator's voice, which is structured by the absent author and related to the woman writing in Elvedon, then Bernard's identity is from the first word an identity dependent on others and upon contextualization.

Identity in *The Waves,* as in contemporary thought in general, is a category of relationship, not one of a monistic substance.[2] "Bernard" is rendered recognizable only by the likenesses and differences between his perception and tone of voice and those of the other five characters, and he therefore becomes a carefully constructed "shape" of the meta-

1.   The first words of the novel, *"The sun,"* along with Bernard's first image, a "loop of light," set this work firmly in the center of the tradition of western metaphysics so trenchantly critiqued by, among many others, Heidegger and Derrida. Bernard's childhood image, writes Beverly Schlack, links him with Dante and Bernard of Clairvaux, in addition to Henry Vaughan (see *Continuing Presences,* 102 and 151). In this sense, Woolf's novel is modernist. With her insistence on the medium of language and the ways in which it forms and unforms identity, however, she drifts toward the postmodernist.

This distinction in itself is not of great concern for my thinking about *The Waves,* but the abundance of light in the novel does link it with the metaphysics of Narcissus through the images of the sun and the eye, those emblems of being and truth. As Woolf writes, *"Rimmed in a gold circle the looking-glass held the scene immobile as if everlasting in its eye"* (321).

2.   The nineteenth and twentieth centuries' shift from thinking about substantiality to thinking about relationality, a shift that could be copiously documented, stands at the "center" of deconstruction and its philosophical kin. As Derrida says, "Everything begins with structure, configuration, or relationship" (SSP, 286). Although the *différance* upon which relationality depends is currently much touted, and deservedly so, it has much older analogues in Heraclitus and Buddhism, to name but two. And although it is finally unfair to let Michel Foucault represent the entire range of poststructuralism, I will nonetheless note that, as Uta Schaub has written, Foucault "has walked a narrow line between play and purpose, between pure sophistry and the praxis of Oriental schools such as Zen and its early predecessor, the Madhyamikas' *sunyavada*" (315). In Buddhism, the forms give way to the void, much as Woolf hopes language will give way to silence in *The Waves.*

phorical and metonymical play of language. Such an existence, which we all share as textualized subjects who live in the medium of the symbolic, must surrender the hope of a "final summing up," though not of a moment of authentic speech as defined by Lacan (which by its nature cannot last). Bernard, with Rhoda as his primary foil, enacts the tension between these two visions.

Bernard can attempt to "find a meaning" because he is a poet, and a poet is one who recognizes that he is made up of the others while simultaneously retaining a sense of distinctiveness from the others. "I do not believe in separation," he tells us. "We are not single" (221). Soon, thereafter, at college, he continues his meditation on his identity:

> "What am I? I ask. This? No, I am that. Especially now, when I have left a room, and people talking, and the stone flags ring out with my solitary footsteps, and I behold the moon rising, sublimely, indifferently, over the ancient chapel—then it becomes clear that I am not one and simple, but complex and many.... They do not understand that I have to effect different transitions; have to cover the entrances and exits of several different men who alternately act their parts as Bernard." (227)

Bernard understands the many-voiced plurality of the psyche, as well as its theatrical nature; he understands, that is, the fact that the multiple facets of a personality must be acted out and dramatized on the stage of a life. The various roles that Bernard knows himself to be playing, however, do not fly asunder and become centers of autonomous behavior or discourse, a situation tantamount to psychosis. There is, for the most part, an ongoing connection between the "personalities" that form Bernard; he continues, that is, to possess an ego, a psychic function that reassures him that his I is one self and not another. And this sense of unity is accomplished primarily through his imagination and the act of writing.

From very early in the novel, Bernard is established as a writer, as an inventor of stories: "We melt into each other with phrases" (185), he confides to Susan, as he shows her the "mythical kingdom" (Boone, 629) of Elvedon, where the "lady sits between the two long windows, writing" (186). The merging of selves—such as that of reader and writer, analyst and analysand—that language enables to occur is for Bernard, at least for most of the novel, not a final loss of a separate ego. His ego does, however, often identify with an other as his own way of seeking for a stable place in the world.

For instance, he is incessantly making notes under different letters of
the alphabet for his future book, a work that "will certainly run to many
volumes embracing every known variety of man and woman" (221), and
at one point he quotes his own future biographer. In order to write a
love note to a woman, he attempts to mold his style to that of Byron.
"Yet," he finally confesses to himself, "it falls flat. It peters out. I cannot
get up steam enough to carry me over the transition. My true self breaks
off from my assumed" (229).

The conflict is clear. In order to invent himself as a writer, Bernard
must first establish an identification with writers, whether the object of
his identification is a fantasy image of his future self (complete with
biographer) or an already canonized poet such as Byron. On the other
hand, if he is to become a writer in actuality, and not merely in fantasy, he
must pass through such identifications and create his own works, his
own style. He must transform his note taking, however perspicacious it
may be, into a work of art. Identifications must be broken for artistic
production to begin.

But, for Bernard, his first response to the loss of identifications is
abjection:

> "The truth is that I need the stimulus of other people. Alone, over
> my dead fire, I tend to see the thin places in my own stories. The
> real novelist, the perfectly simple human being, could go on,
> indefinitely, imagining. He would not integrate, as I do. He would
> not have this devastating sense of grey ashes in a burnt-out grate.
> Some blind flaps in my eyes. Everything becomes impervious. I
> cease to invent." (230)

In the face of a fantasied "perfect" novelist—God, for instance?—who
goes on imagining forever, Bernard, with the fires of his libidinal engage-
ment with others already dead, sees only his own failures and his inability to maintain the force of his fiction making.

Entering into the territory of abjection, we come upon depression and
despair, what Julia Kristeva has called the "hidden face of Narcissus" (MI,
106). When Bernard is uninspired by the presence of others, the fire of
his libido burns down into the ashes of despair, but this moment remains
true to the psychic contours of his artistic nature, even though he himself cannot, at the moment of abjection, be cognizant of this. His power
to symbolize, driven in large part by his cathexis of others, periodically
collapses upon itself, and in the image of this collapse, the shadow of
Narcissus is discovered. The loss of love—and what is love from a psy-

choanalytic perspective other than object cathexis?—causes the long, slow fall into a depression in which literary creation cannot occur.

As Freud demonstrated in "On Narcissism," the loss of love and interest in the world is characteristic of the schizophrenic, whose suffering is that the many voices of the psyche are unmoored from the anchoring power of the ego (Lacan's *points de capiton*). Bernard does not, however, lapse into schizophrenia, for in his wish to "sum up" and "give meaning" to the moments of experience recounted in the novel, Bernard serves as the proxy ego of *The Waves*. His "writing" binds the voices into a story, and the threat that otherness will dissolve the unity of the ego is overcome by rhetorical action. Nonetheless, such action is not an omnipotent talisman against dissolution; as a representative of Narcissus, Bernard exists tenuously on the borderline between speech and its constitutive condition, emptiness.

This emptiness—as the Saussurean bar between signifier and signified, as the arbitrariness of the sign, and as the "gaping mirror" of Lacan—is both the necessary ground as well as the perduring menace of narcissistic identity and the existence of a stable ego. As Kristeva says, "Narcissism protects emptiness, causes it to exist, and thus, as lining of that emptiness, insures an elementary separation. Without that solidarity between emptiness and narcissism, chaos would sweep away any possibility of distinction, trace, and symbolization, which would in turn confuse the limits of the body, words, the real, and the symbolic" (TL, 24). To write a coherent narrative, a story, the arbitrary must be balanced by the rigorously ordered, and difference must be complemented by the repetition of the same.

And yet, at times, the story that Bernard is perpetually writing evaporates into the nothingness from which it emerges, and writing, for him, stops. As a subject, he dies. This occurs when his overidentifications with a figure such as Byron break apart and he is left to his own true, though not omnipotent or grandiose, self. Neville, who is fully aware of his friend's imitations of Tolstoi, Meredith, or Byron, leaves Bernard a copy of a poem. Bernard's response is to feel torn from his artistic models and stripped down to an essential, fragile self. "All semblances were rolled up. 'You are not Byron; you are yourself.' To be contracted by another person into a single being—how strange" (236). The psychological inflation of being *like* Byron is replaced by the deflation entailed by the loss of the master model and the affective realization that one is only oneself: finite, awash in ambiguity, and more of a note taker than a grand Byronic crusader. But it is only at this nadir of depression that Bernard might indeed discover his own capabilities as a writer.

There are other occasions when Bernard crosses the gap at the borders between speech and silence, identity and nothingness. When, at a
dinner party to bid farewell to Percival, Bernard engages in a long meditation upon his upcoming marriage, he says of himself that "having
dropped off satisfied like a child from the breast, I am at liberty now to
sink down, deep, into what passes, this omnipresent, general life" (253).

Nietzsche's description of the Dionysian experience and Freud's discussion of the "feeling of an indissoluble bond, of being one with the
external world as a whole" (*Civilization*, 12), are apropos here, but
Bernard is not able to remain for long in the cocoon of the general life.
All too soon, personal identity, with its many strictures, reappears: "Yet
behold, it returns. One cannot extinguish that persistent smell. It steals
in through some crack in the structure—one's identity. I am not part of
the street—no, I observe the street. One splits off, therefore" (254).
After briefly "traversing the sunless territory of nonidentity," Bernard
acknowledges that "to be myself (I note) I need the illumination of other
people's eyes, and therefore cannot be entirely sure what is my self"
(255).

Bernard's acknowledgment is an elegantly succinct statement of
Lacan's thesis—built upon the fundamental perceptions of Hegel, Saussure, and Freud—that since otherness is always prior to psychological and
social reality, "identity" is inevitably a misnomer. Nonidentity is dark and
sunless for Bernard because it is only the sun, throughout the history of
metaphysics and literature, that facilitates the Eye of appearance and that
engenders the I of identity, a movement that sets us once again firmly in
the fantasy of Narcissus peering into the reflections of the pool.

As Lacan says of the gaze, "I see only from one point, but in my
existence I am looked at from all sides"; and that "which makes us
consciousness institutes us by the same token as *speculum mundi*"
(FFC, 72, 75). We come into existence only as beings who are being seen
from the standpoint of the other; then, through the intricate reflective
interplay of the subject within the mirrors of others, we develop an
identity. Bernard is right when he admits that he needs the "illumination"
of other people's eyes, for it is those others who draw him from the
shadows of nonidentity into the light of identity.

But even at noontide, when the self is most certain of itself—perhaps
a zenith briefly achieved with Descartes—there is darkness on the other
side of the world, and the waves continue to sweep onto the shore. In
the passage that I have been discussing, Bernard's identity returns (as a
"smell"), but it will continue to fluctuate between sufficient speech and

silence until, toward the end of the novel, he experiences the loss of both himself and his book.

Before I examine that final loss, however, I will examine Rhoda's descriptions of her experience, for not only does she know the allure of nothingness, but she at last throws herself suicidally into that abyss. Rhoda has great difficulty with words and is, in some ways, Bernard's opposite. She is a woman for whom writing cannot play a redemptive and protective role against the incessant waves of existence. The lining provided by the narcissistic sheath of the ego fails her.

However, like Bernard, Rhoda is acutely aware of her relationship with others. But whereas he can use those connections to call himself into existence and invent stories, Rhoda knows only a final exclusion from the community of friends. For her, the waves, the mirror, and nothingness merge into one unreadable blankness that cannot support identity. As she "puts off [her] hopeless desire to be Susan, to be Jinny," she cries,

> "Oh, to awake from dreaming! Look, there is the chest of draw-
> ers. Let me pull myself out of these waters. But they heap them-
> selves on me; they sweep me between their great shoulders; I
> am turned; I am tumbled; I am stretched, among these long
> lights, these long waves, these endless paths, with people pursu-
> ing, pursuing." (193)

Rhoda's I is "turned," "tumbled," and "stretched"; her identity never settles into the smooth plane of adequate reflection from the mirror of the world—and by implication the mirror of the mother—and therefore is continually being whirled around. Since there is not an adequate mirroring and a subsequent coalescence of the same, which would support a more adaptive ego, she exhibits a form of paranoia and fears the presence of others: they annihilate rather than cocreate her sense of her own subjectivity.

Rhoda, who attaches herself to names "like amulets against disaster," comments that "I hate looking-glasses which show me my real face. Alone, I often fall down into nothingness" (204). Because she does not have a sufficient experience of mirroring from the external world of others, Rhoda also does not experience a cohesive mirroring of the world within, of the internal representations of herself without which there can be no stable ego. The entire psychological dialectic of inward and outward upon which identity depends becomes disrupted; the

waves of perception, of affect, of Kristeva's semiotic, shatter the image in
the mirror.

On the first day of summer holidays, Rhoda comes to a puddle and
stands before its superficial depths, terrified. "I could not cross it. Identity failed me. We are nothing, I said, and fell" (219). She manages, finally,
to cross the "cadaverous space" of the puddle—death by water—then
says that "with intermittent shocks, sudden as the springs of a tiger, life
emerges heaving its dark crest from the sea. It is to this we are attached; it is to this we are bound, as bodies to wild horses. And yet we
have invented devices for filling up the crevices and disguising these
fissures" (219). Metaphor seems to be running amok. Life is a tiger that
springs from the sea; the tiger becomes a horse; and, suddenly, the sea
becomes a fissured earth. (Perhaps Poseidon, Earth shaker and ruler of
horses long before he entered the sea, lives in the depths of this watery
earth?)

Rhoda's metaphorical consciousness comes very close to a total disen-
gagement from any referentiality or intersubjective purposefulness. Her
consciousness, in other words, verges on losing the power of what Lacan
has called the "anchoring points," the "knots which anticipatorily tie
meaning down through a diachronic function of the signified" (Ragland-
Sullivan, JL, 229), a process by which the personal language of the *moi*
hooks onto the shared, culturally conditioned language of the *je*. Without the anchoring points of discourse, there is nothing to stabilize the
narcissistically fixed ego, and the subject careens into the fissures, the
cadaverous space of death and dissolution of identity, entailed by the
construction of the subject in the first place.

Rhoda falls; her manner of existence is to whirl and fall away from
herself and from others. She is "broken into separate pieces" (248), and,
as she says, she "cannot make one moment merge in the next. To me
they are all violent, all separate; and if I fall under the shock of the leap of
the moment you will be on me, tearing me to pieces. I have no end in
view" (265). What terrifies Rhoda, being torn to pieces by the tiger of
existence, has in fact already occurred in her psyche, for she was never
stitched together strongly enough to be torn apart. She has always been a
shattered sentence, a sentence without punctuation and without an
"end" in view. As Ragland-Sullivan observes, "Lacan viewed the sentence
as a perfect model of the kind of anticipatory/retroactive combination
which makes up the 'self' as a unit of narcissistic meaning [and] only
with the last term is the suspense resolved, the meaning of the sentence
made complete" (JL, 230). Rhoda's life has neither a period nor an

ellipsis to conclude its passage; rather, it breaks into the chaos of its constituent parts.

This break is imagined either as a falling into the cadaverous space of any object in the world or as the recurring image of a tiger, teeth bared, leaping always at her throat. Nietzsche also knew something about the teeth of this tiger and about nothingness. As he says:

> [Nature] threw away the key; and woe to the calamitous curiosity which might peer just once through a crack in the chamber of consciousness and look down, and sense that man rests upon the merciless, the greedy, the insatiable, the murderous, in the indif-ference of his ignorance—hanging in dreams, as it were, upon the back of a tiger. ("On Truth and Lies," 217)[3]

Rhoda has just such a calamitous curiosity, and often peers vertiginously through the cracks of consciousness at the tiger, who is always in motion, who leaps beneath the useful ruse of identity and its analogue, namely the determinable and determined text. Bernard's friend dwells close to what Freud called the primary processes, in which psychic energy remains unbound, flowing freely from one metaphorical image to the next without regard for the fitting together entailed by the trivium of logic, rhetoric, and grammar. Rhoda, unlike Bernard, does not have the capacity to interpret; rather, she is drawn irrevocably into her vision of the infinite pool of reflected images that, for her, finally reflects only nothingness disguised as the things of the world.

As she gazes out over the sea, Rhoda admits that she sees and touches nothing. "We may sink," she muses, "and settle on the waves. The sea will drum in my ears. . . . Rolling me over the waves will shoulder me under. Everything falls in a tremendous shower, dissolving me" (319). Rhoda does indeed show us depression and melancholy, the "hidden face of Narcissus," but she does not proceed to erect the "fetish of the work of art . . . in disavowal of this mobilizing affliction" (Kristeva, MI, 105). It is precisely this form of fetishization, with its simultaneous admission of and resistance to the fracturing loss of the object of love, that is left for Bernard.

In the ninth and final section of the novel, "the looking-glass was pale as the mouth of a cave shadowed by hanging creepers" (340); the mirror

---

3. Nietzsche's short text continues to amaze me with its extraordinary compression of what has been elaborated by psychoanalysis and poststructuralist philosophy.

of writing and representation opens up into the unknown depths, one of
the traditional locations for the home of meaning.[4] Bernard sits down to
eat with a listener he has met only once, in passing, to explain the
meaning of his life. Suddenly, the other of the intersubjective speaking
circuit is present; the I has discovered a "you," and perhaps full speech of
dialogue can at last replace the homogeneity of the six soliloquies.

But the you addressed by Bernard never *appears* in the text; we have
no visual or auditory image of the person who sits across the table from
Bernard, apparently listening so patiently to his ruminations. The only
sign of the listener's existence is that he or she becomes an addressee of
Bernard's discourse. Benveniste has said of this necessary other of discourse that "consciousness of self is only possible if it is experienced by
contrast. I use *I* only when I am speaking to someone who will be a *you*
in my address (even if the 'you' is only my objectified 'I'). It is this
condition of dialogue that is constitutive of *person,* for it implies that
reciprocally *I* becomes *you* in the address of the one who in his turn
designates himself as *I*" (225). Since the copresence of a you and an I are
necessary for self-consciousness, a you must have been present since the
beginning of *The Waves,* not just in the final section in which a you is,
however vaguely, incarnated into the text as Bernard's listener.

The implicit you of the six characters' monologues is the "objectified I"
of each character as he or she listens to his or her interior soliloquy (the
speech of thought is a self-reflexive act), and the position of implied
addressee is also taken by the characters for each other (the speakers take
each other into account, fantasize responses from the others). Finally, the
you is the reader who "listens" so attentively to the discourse of the six
friends. The "exterior" other to Bernard's I, then, becomes his "*echo* to
whom [he] says *you* and who says *you* to [him]" (Benveniste, 225; emphasis added). The reader is constructed as an intersubjective partner, an
echoing other.

4. The depths are the "home" of meaning for an entire hermeneutical tradition. For
example, in many myths and fairy tales, the "treasure" is found at the bottom of the sea or in
caves. More self-conscious writing includes Romantic poetry ("In Xanadu did Kubla Khan / A
stately pleasure dome decree: / Where Alph, the sacred river, ran / Through caverns measure-
less to man / Down to a sunless sea"), depth psychology (". . . my first obligation was to probe
the depths of my own psyche" [Jung, *Memories, Dreams, Reflections,* 176]), and the depth
theology of Paul Tillich (who writes in *Shaking the Foundations* that "the name of this infinite
and inexhaustible depth and ground of all being is *God.* That depth is what the word *God*
means" [57]). The transformation from images of the depths to those of the surface, which I
traced briefly in my introduction, is one of the signs of postmodernism and the presence of
narcissism. In *The Waves,* the depths have an ambivalent character as place of both a source of
meaning and a disintegration of meaning.

As interpretive readers, we sit across from Bernard, following his phrases, wondering with him whether language has the capacity for telling any true stories, and struggling with the possibility that "life is not susceptible perhaps to the treatment we give it when we try to tell it" (362). Can language, in other words, constitute an I that can adequately perceive, or create, the real? Like Rhoda, Bernard exists at the edge of the abyss that runs like a fault between the signifier, the signified, and the referent. Both are divided subjects, but while Rhoda falls, Bernard keeps speaking.

As Bernard speaks, as he searches for the right word, his identity composes and decomposes. As he considers his past self, he remembers that "I made notes for stories; drew portraits in the margin of my pocket-book and thus became still more separate" (344). And later, in his dialogue with the silent listener, he notes that "I have seen so many different things, have made so many different sentences" (377). Each sentence that Bernard has scribbled, each note that he has taken to catch the quick flash of insight, marked a separation both from the event itself and from all the other possible expressions of the event. Each thing with its attached word—clock, ring, street—divides the world into separate units.

Bernard's life was organized around the hope that writing would be a medium of that which is "beyond and outside our own predicament . . . that which is symbolic, and thus perhaps permanent" (349). But by the time he comes to his grand summary, language has become more problematic. Neither grammar and syntax nor the conventions of high society can sufficiently order the flux of existence. "But it is a mistake," Bernard says,

> "this extreme precision, this orderly and military progress; a convenience, a lie. There is always deep below it, even when we arrive punctually at the appointed time with our white waistcoats and polite formalities, a rushing stream of broken dreams, nursery rhymes, street cries, half-finished sentences and sights—elm trees, willow trees, gardeners sweeping, women writing—that rise and sink even as we hand a lady down to dinner." (353–54)

In his description of the "rushing stream," which is strikingly reminiscent of Lacan's sense of the language that is the unconscious, Bernard admits the fragmented nature of language—it gets broken off in midsentence—and how fantasies of childhood subsist beneath adult ego-consciousness.

Just after recalling another image of the woman at Elvedon, Bernard
declares that "I took my mind, my being, the old dejected, almost inani-
mate object and lashed it about among these odds and ends, sticks and
straws, detestable little bits of wreckage, flotsam and jetsam, floating on
the oily surface" (363). He takes the wreckage of his psyche and,
through language, brings order to the flux. The word is the link between
psyche and world. "I netted them under with a sudden phrase. I re-
trieved them from formlessness with words" (364). But the wreckage
remains, transmogrified into a language that is inevitably unstable, that
feverishly searches for a motionless vantage point, and that is ruptured
by the power of the real. The mind is not a polished mirror into which
Narcissus can gaze in self-satisfied rapture; it is an "oily surface" that
flattens and distorts all that comes within its borders.

Two of Bernard's images, however, may be strong enough to withstand the formlessness that threatens all language and identity. The first,
perhaps his earliest memory and one that reappears often throughout his
life, is the scene at Elvedon where the gardeners are sweeping and the
woman is writing. Joseph Boone has suggested that Elvedon is an aspect
of Bernard's "recognition that 'I am myself' " and perhaps even of "part of
his preconscious history *preceding* identity" (633). Although the stabil-
ity and content of the image seem to me to place it firmly within the
symbolic stage rather than the preceding mirror stage, I agree with
Boone about Elvedon's centrality to Bernard's sense of himself and his
separation from others. "Sitting at the core of his subconscious in a
primeval setting is his mother; sweeping away the obscuring leaves of
ordinary experiences, the gardeners prepare the way for this visionary
glimpse of the deep truth residing at the core of Bernard's being"
(Boone, 634).

Bernard himself is struck by the unusual persistence of this image:

> "Down below, through the depths of the leaves, the gardeners
> swept the lawns with great brooms. The lady sat writing. Trans-
> fixed, stopped dead, I thought, 'I cannot interfere with a single
> stroke of those brooms. They sweep and they sweep. Nor with
> the fixity of that woman writing.' It is strange that one cannot
> stop gardeners sweeping nor dislodge a woman. There they have
> remained all my life." (343)

The woman, writing, is fixed as if eternally. The central image of Bernard's unconscious, then, is of a woman creating through writing. Woolf
births the text that will birth an image of herself writing between two

long windows; within the text, Bernard's mother writes his existence; and, in his turn, Bernard writes the final text of the sextet of friends. Writing spins forth the world and brings forth its originary moment into the chiaroscuro of the tale itself.

The writing of identity, however, brings its own wreckage along with it. The image of the woman in Elvedon, which is "stopped dead" through a process of psychological mummification, dissipates when exposed to the corrosive forces of Bernard's experience of life. The woman at Elvedon cannot, finally, act as a version of an archetypal and stable signified through which Bernard might understand and master the question of his identity. Although a lifelong mimesis of the woman writing provides Bernard with a relatively enduring narcissistic fixation around which to organize a coherent narrative of his existence, the power of the fixation eventually erodes.

After the old image of Elvedon has emerged once again from his mind, Bernard sweeps it impatiently away: "Now what situation was there to end? Dullness and doom. And what to explore? The leaves and the wood concealed nothing. If a bird rose I should no longer make a poem—I should repeat what I had said before" (363). Where the leaves of the mind once concealed an entire kingdom of the imagination, now there is no secret world, no mysterious depths that will reveal themselves to the artistic imagination. There is only the nothing and the repetition of that which has been said already. When Bernard's identification with the woman writing snaps apart, the resultant crack in his psyche is opened for the appearance of Thanatos, the death instinct, which is, in Freud's thought, both prior to and beyond the pleasure principle.

The phenomenological consequence of the appearance of death is a profound sense of melancholy, the dark side of the face of Narcissus. "Out we creep," Bernard says wearily, "from the arch of the currant leaves, out into a wider world. The true order of things—this is our perpetual illusion—is now apparent" (365). The true order of things is that things have no order other than that imposed upon them by the net of language that enables the construction of the human world: a narcissistic subject in a world available for narcissistic appropriation.

Language, from this vantage point, is a narcissistic inflation because the other partner in the creation of meaning is nothingness. And that knowledge is no longer sufficient for Bernard: "I, carrying a notebook, making phrases, had recorded merely changes; a shadow, I had been sedulous to take note of shadows. How can I proceed now, I said, without a self, weightless and visionless, through a world weightless, without illusion?" (375). The self and the world, as is always the case, mirror one another; and here the mirroring is only the depressing vertigo of emptiness reflecting emptiness.

And the book, that record of the innumerable records of the written life, shares the fate of the self and the world: "My book, stuffed with phrases, has dropped to the floor. It lies under the table to be swept up by the charwoman when she comes wearily at dawn looking for scraps of paper, old tram tickets, and here and there a note screwed into a ball and left with the litter to be swept up" (381). Writing, which begins in the "rag and bone shop of the heart," completes its circle and returns to the scrap heap. The self decomposes into the sounds that preceded the symbolic order of language: a growl, a chirp, a cry, the hiss of waves on the shore.

Once the illusion of impermeable selfhood and the definitive book has vanished, what does one do? Bernard, out of both habit and courage, keeps speaking—though now not to his seated listener but only to the invisible reader—and as his final performance in the face of death, he dons the mask of Percival, the heroic warrior. As Boone notes, "Elvedon will finally become the equivalent of Bernard's own private language— the 'howl' or 'cry' he seeks when phrases fail, when he hurls his final defiance at Death on the last page of the novel" (635). The image of Elvedon first dissolves into a private language, a language unsuitable for literature or communication, which is then replaced with the image of Percival charging against death.

Percival, a figure without a voice in the novel, emerges with Bernard's last words to become the central emblem of the novel. As an absence, he had structured the lives of his friends, who loved and admired him; as a sudden presence, a presence brought to life only by Bernard's identification with him, he usurps the voices of the other six, even Bernard's, and gains an unexpected privilege of place. The woman writing has been strangely transformed into the futile but heroic warrior who rides against death: "Death is the enemy. It is death against whom I ride with my spear couched and my hair flying back like a young man's, like Percival's, when he galloped in India. I strike spurs into my horse. Against you I will fling myself, unvanquished and unyielding, O Death!" (383). Very nice sentiments indeed, but Percival was killed in India when his horse tripped in a molehill; death is not daunted by a knight on a horse, even if that knight be Percival himself. As Susan Dick has argued, however, perhaps Bernard's passion is ultimately a statement of the paradoxical triumph of the artist, "for we know that Bernard makes this grand gesture of defiance with the knowledge of his inevitable defeat.

Like the artist, he commits himself to his illusion, knowing it is an illusion" (50).

But we know that Bernard has experienced a diminution of the power of the woman writing at Elvedon, a loss of the self he has familiarly called I, and a loss of his notebook, which marks him as a writer. Although his personal voice had been underwritten by the woman writing, it is, at the conclusion of *The Waves,* overcome by Percival and the conventions of Western culture. Byron, whom Bernard had rejected in order to discover himself as a writer, returns with a vengeance in the form of a knight of the Holy Grail who makes a vain charge against death.

Earlier in the novel, at the dinner where the six friends celebrate Percival's departure for India, Bernard imagines that "by applying the standards of the West, by using the violent language that is natural to him [Percival], the bullock-cart is righted in less than five minutes. The Oriental problem is solved. He rides on; the multitude cluster round him regarding him as if he were—what indeed he is—a God" (269). After Percival's death in India, Bernard reflects that "about him my feeling was: he sat there in the centre. Now I go to that spot no longer. The place is empty" (282). Bernard, however, cannot resist eventually filling the emptiness left by Percival's death.

In this context, I will do no more than cursorily invoke Derrida's work on absence and presence, the centered and the uncentered, but if "the absence of the transcendental signified extends the domain and the play of signification infinitely" (SSP, 280), then the abrupt presence of Percival as a godlike figure who "solves" the Oriental problem with the "violent" language of the Occident would put an end to signification. This is precisely what occurs when Bernard capitulates to the image of Percival as it returns, as it were, from the dead. The play of signification that constitutes writing stops, and we are left with only the final six words: "*The waves broke on the shore*" (383).

When writing stops, within the metaphorical context within which we are viewing the self and the text, self-composition stops as well. Bernard's heroic gesture against death is actually, and already, the utter catastrophe of having succumbed to death. If, as Lacan and others have argued, a kind of death is the beginning of writing, then writing remains faithful to its origins and returns to the collapse of language and its correlate, the unified and narcissistic self. The emptiness, which narcissism attempts so valiantly to forget, erupts to destroy the fortress of the ego.

In *The Waves* the project of Narcissus, to construct an identity through the power of language and thereby defeat nothingness, fails. The voice of Narcissus, Bernard and his friends, who attempt to order the world through phrases and stories, falls silent, but only after rendering the world for a moment luminous. This is their achievement, but nonetheless it is an achievement that cannot withstand the waves that surge up to break the reflective mirror of narcissistic art. The pool of Narcissus, unable to provide a place in which to represent the other, becomes a cavern of soliloquies; it becomes a sea of waves, broken and churned, that drowns all who wish for the serenity and self-possession of the self in love with its own image.

5

The Mirror of Narcissus:
Pathology and Symbolic Ballast
in *The Ogre*

The world of the perverse is a world without others, therefore
it is a world without possibility.
—Gilles Deleuze

Michel Tournier's *The Ogre* is a
novel of signs about signs and the implications of signs. In the novel's
opening section, the "Sinister Writings of Abel Tiffauges," we are introduced to a protagonist who narratively constructs a narcissistic network
of signs that eventually destroys its creator. Tiffauges's pathological process of radically narcissistic symbolization, which mirrors the apocalyptic culture of the Third Reich, draws us directly into the crater of his
collapsing, sign-haunted psyche as well as into further explorations of
how the subject positions itself in relation to an other.

At the conclusion of *The Ogre,* Tiffauges, who is carrying a survivor of
Auschwitz on his shoulders, sinks into the viscous black mud of the
Prussian swampland. If we are not unwittingly to emulate him and sink
into the marsh of signs that is the novel—that is, if we are to contend
that the novel as a field of signs holds any possibility other than an
engulfing self-referentiality of both writer and reader—we must read
with an eye for the distinctions between metaphor and absolute identification. We must attempt to clarify the dialectic between sign and psyche,
each a foundational metaphor that implies the other, and see how a
narcissistic semiosis drives itself inexorably toward the swamp.

Psychoanalyis and semiotics have long been integrally bound up with one another. At the outset of modern semiotics, Saussure remarked that *"a science that studies the life of signs within society* is conceivable; it would be a part of social psychology and consequently of general psychology" (16), and the development of Lacan's thought has proven the fertility of the union of the disciplines. The psyche, as I have been contending, is always signed; signs are always psychicized.

Human beings are always adrift in the semiotic susurrus, and we are all implicated in the intersubjectivity of the transferential relations among reader, writer, and text. But all drifting, all the roles that metaphor might play within and between psyches and texts, is not identical. In this reading of *The Ogre,* I will attend closely to Tiffauges's search for an anchoring point that might act as ballast to ground his identity within the shifting currents of his symbol system.

Tiffauges himself loses his connections with a common *logos* and develops a form of psychosis that makes claim to a mystical, because totalizing and participatory, intuition. "All is sign" (5) he declares, and when we realize that all the signs are, for him, primarily implicated in revealing his own destiny, we immediately recognize the link between the vertiginously narcissistic disposition of his psyche and the annihilation of any socially objectified meaning. If "all is one," then the ego has ceased to exercise its function of discriminating between differences.

Tiffauges takes his symbolic creations literally rather than metaphorically and therefore fails to draw any distinctions between personal experience and the events of World War II that ensnare and eventually swallow the ogre for whom eating is so vital. The novel opens with lines written by Abel on 3 January 1938:

> You're an ogre, Rachel used to say to me sometimes. An ogre? A fabulous monster emerging from the mists of time? Well, yes, I do think there's something magical about me, I do think there's a secret collusion, deep down, connecting what happens to me with what happens in general, and enabling my particular history to bend the course of things in its own direction. (3)

Tiffauges's self-understanding is woven neither from a rational foundation—from a mediating position that maintains the tension between individual and collective history—nor from the basis of society's conventional signs (which are themselves, as he realizes, corrupt and death dealing), but from a pathological imagination that reaches toward an apocalyptic finality. It is this unsettling conjunction between an imagination that mechanically churns out portentous signs and Tiffauges's absolute *belief* in his created fictions that raises the question of the psychogenesis and development of narcissism.

At what psychological node does narcissism "originate" for Tiffauges? How, in the later phases of its expressive unfolding, does a self-referential vision of existence show itself? The psychoanalytical *locus classicus* that serves as an initial point of departure for these questions is, once again, Freud's 1914 essay "On Narcissism." In this essay Freud comes to the conclusion that the "narcissism which arises when libidinal cathexes are called in away from external objects must be conceived of as a secondary form, superimposed upon a primary one that is obscured by manifold influences" (32).

But that which is superimposed, the formations of secondary narcissism that involve a withdrawal of energy from objects in the world, is for Freud always informed by the deeper, more archaic strata of the psyche in which primary narcissism is constellated. The division between the two forms is, therefore, finally a provisional classification, although it is only through the "manifold influences," the representations, of the secondary phenomena that we are able to trace our path back to the primary level of experience that is fundamentally inarticulate until after the fact. Symbolization is deferred, but once the symbolic network is operative, we can follow an *epistrophic* course back and down into the earlier organizations of the psyche.

Primary narcissism, a stage of development that exists before the entrance through the looking-glass into the symbolic world of language and culture, is the nonreflective experience of cathecting the ego, rather than an external object, with one's reserve of libido. Freud postulates a narcissistic component that is constitutive of the personality and that in some becomes the determining power of the choice of love objects. Such is the case with Tiffauges, who is unable to escape the gravitational pull of that primitive, inchoate psychic organization called primary narcissism.

Freud establishes that the narcissist is unable to make a choice for an other as a love object, for such a choice involves a distinction between the self and the other as well as a capacity to continue to maintain a dialectic between separateness and commonality with an other. For a narcissist like Tiffauges, however, since everything is ordered through a "logic" of self-referentiality, everything becomes totalized into a monolithic system of signs. No psychic space within his world is reserved for the presence of an other.

Instead of the psychic operation of individuation and the ability to recognize the tension of differences within metaphorical likenesses, the narcissist regresses to the earliest stage of psychic development, a stage of *identifications.* Freud remarks of this phase—and "phase" can be an ongoing, repetitive moment of psychological life—that "the ego wishes to incorporate this object into itself and the method by which it would do so, in this oral or cannibalistic stage, is by devouring it" ("Mourning and Melancholia," 160). Tiffauges, like Hitler and Goering, is described as an ogre; and orality, with its devouring need, dominates his fantasy life.

As he confesses, "When I say I love meat and blood and flesh the only thing that matters is the word 'love.' I am all love" (67). Meat, blood, and flesh are all sublimated into love, but the love is always the love of an ogre, a flesh eater. Later in the novel, when Tiffauges is placed in charge of the boys at Kaltenborn, an S.S. training school, he declares that "all these children were being boiled in a giant cauldron before being eaten, but I had thrown myself in through love and was cooking with them" (328). The devourer and devoured will be annihilated together; Tiffauges, as ogre, eats—but he recognizes that he is the eaten as well.

Abel hungrily devours the potential objects of his love; and by examining the figures that he "chooses" as the primal dramatis personae of his fantasy life, the introjected objects of his love, we can reconstruct the unconscious configuration that underlies his narcissistic creation of a world of delusions. Most of Tiffauges's identifications are with characters from mythological, legendary, and historical narratives. Even when they are chosen from a more immediate sphere, however, they are soon inflated to a mythic dimension. Abel constructs his personal "pantheon" by "leafing through dictionaries, picking up what I could in textbooks, watching out for fleeting allusions to what really interested me in French or history lessons" (10). The textual self, myopically enlarged, is being pasted together.

Three primary identifications—with Nestor, a horse named Bluebeard, and the Erl-King—most clearly reveal the sources and mechanisms of the psychic breakdown that Tiffauges suffers. Nestor, the janitor's son and a denizen of the "underworld" of St. Christopher's Academy, is the most direct inspiration for Tiffauges's "Sinister Writings," the first-person narrative that is begun before his capture by the Germans and that is eventually resumed when he takes up residence at Kaltenborn.

When Rachel, the object of a short-lived affair, calls him an ogre, Abel recalls "the ghost of a monstrous child, both terrifyingly precocious and disconcertingly infantile" (9). It is the image of Nestor, this powerful revenant, that returns from the past to take "sovereign and irrestible possession" of Tiffauges. The components of Nestor's personality are the very same ones stressed by Abel in his self-descriptions; in fact, the latter claims to have been "derived" from his friend.

Even as he writes his sinister script, he is being written by a ghost-writer who is felt to be the source of his "true" self. "I thus have two sets of writing," Tiffauges comments. "One that is 'adroit,' pleasant, social, commercial, reflecting the masked character I pretend to be in the eyes of society; and one that is 'sinister,' distorted by all the 'gauchenesses' of genius, full of flashes and cries—in short, inhabited by the spirit of Nestor" (30). The left hand, like the unconscious, sees what the right hand cannot. To write outside of the conventions of society, the left hand must be guided by a ghost. (As we have seen, Bernard calls upon a ghost at the conclusion of *The Waves,* and as we shall see in the next chapter, Daniel Martin revives a number of ghosts to write the story of himself in his eponymous novel.)

Nestor is the mage of Abel's adolescence, and as such, he transmits esoteric knowledge to his pupil.[1] The most essential of these teachings concerns *la phorie,* the capacity to lift up and carry, and, especially, the capacity to read signs, an art that demands a familiarity with the myster-ies of the meta*phor:* "Signs and the deciphering of signs. What signs? And what did their deciphering reveal? If I could answer that question my whole life would be changed, and not only my life but also—I dare write it because I know no one will ever read these lines—the course of history" (21).

Abel believes that the key to his destiny lies in his ability to read signs and that the revelation of signs has the power to change both individual and collective history. Lacan, among others, agrees: the "slightest alter-ation in the relation between man and the signifier . . . changes the whole course of history by modifying the moorings that anchor his being" (E, 174). But the psychogenesis and development of Abel's symbolic con-struct lead not to liberation but, instead, into a blind slavery to un-ballasted signs, to a "malign inversion" of the poetic wisdom that is genuinely able to decipher, or at least raise the question about how we might decipher, the hieroglyphs of the world.

---

1.   Susan Petit discusses the historical dimension of this character and his place in the novel. "The Nestorian Heresy," she writes, "is at the origin of both the theme of the divided self and the idea of carrying, or *la phorie,* in this novel. To begin with the latter idea, not only could one think of Jesus in Nestorian doctrine as 'carrying' the divine Word, but one of the key issues in the Nestorian controversy had to do with whether one could call Mary *Theotokos,* carrier of God. Significantly, in the novel, Tiffauges' desire to carry others is traceable to Nestor, who carries Tiffauges on his shoulders in a game at school and discovers that 'porter un enfant' is 'une chose si belle' " (235).

In addition to teaching Tiffauges the general science of semiotics, an idiosyncratic version of that science to be sure, Nestor also alerts his student to the presence of the two master signs of creation and apocalypse. As Nestor and Abel wander through the dormitory and down to the lavatory at 3 A.M., the giant dwarf remarks that "there must be an absolute alpha-omega sign here somewhere—but where?" (54). Nestor mounts the throne of the toilet and drops his trousers to reveal a tiny penis—he, like Abel, is a "microgenitomorph"—and sits to defecate.

Examining the results, Nestor comments that "tonight omega has been in medieval mood. Look, pretty Fauges—towers and turrets surrounded by a double rampart. Feudal as well as medieval! Last week we performed in flamboyant Gothic" (57). Omega, the transcendental sign of the end, has become radically incarnate in the historicized shapes of shit; or, as Tournier has commented, "Going from philosophy to the novel, ontology becomes scatology: think of the dual definition of 'fundament' " (Delcourt, 25).

Nestor, killed by fire shortly after this strange ritual, is unable to complete Abel's training in the secrets of alpha and omega; that task is left for the pupil to piece together fragment by fragment without the presence of a master of interpretation (though he eventually meets the old commandant of Kaltenborn and Ephraim the Astrophore). Nestor "holds the secret of the obscure complicity linking my fate with the general course of things, manifested first in the fire at St. Christopher's, and since by the almost always trivial outcroppings. They are all warnings, stirring up the deepest, darkest and most secret part of my life, until the time of the Great Tribulation comes which will bring it forth into the light of day" (70). Tiffauges equates self-revelation with the time of the apocalypse; only an event of that magnitude, a world moment in which alpha and omega are incandescently conjoined, will be able to express the deepest recesses of Abel's life. Revelation, for someone living out of the "place" of primary narcissism, comes only with the blinding light of the end of the world, an end that has already occurred and that marks the catastrophic site where the unified ego would have been established.

If Nestor is the primary identification of Abel's adolescence, then Bluebeard becomes the reflection of Tiffauges's psyche once he has been captured by the Germans and sent to the "magic circle" of Rominten, the hunting preserve that was the personal fiefdom of Field Marshal Goering, a semiotician versed in the significances of shit and the "official sacrificer of the Phallophoric Angel" (212). At this point the text is written in the third person—a rhetorical strategy that grants a form of ballast—and speaks eloquently about the naming of the horse:

> For while the pigeons of the Rhine had been first his conquests
> and then his beloved children, it was really himself he was tend-
> ing when he devoted himself to his horse. And it was a revelation,
> this reconciliation with himself, this affection for his own body,
> this still vague tenderness for a man called Abel Tiffauges which
> came to him through the giant gelding from Trakehnen. (223)

Bluebeard is the theriomorphic image of Abel himself. His name evokes
the fictional ancestor of "Barbe-Bleue," a Charles Perrault story that, in
turn, evokes the historical personage of the "real" Bluebeard, Gilles de
Rais, who owned a castle called "Tiffauges."[2]

As for his first name, "Abel" is the brother of Cain, as well as Nestor's
"M'Abel" (44): my pretty and *my* Abel. Within the very morphology of
his name, a web of historical determinants—as fatal as the web woven
for Agamemnon upon his homecoming—binds the character of Abel
Tiffauges. Doomed from birth by his place in the symbolic order, his
narcissistic and sinister writings are his only defense, his futile attempt at
self-assertion against the indifferent brutality of history.

Accompanying the Germans on a hunt, Abel refers to the horse as
"the true source of the new force and conquering youth within him . . .
the giant brother he could feel living between his thighs, who raised
him above the earth and above other men" (227). The horse, an analogue to the camera "lovingly stowed in its genital position" (104)
when Abel, earlier in the novel, hunted children in order to capture
them on film, acts as a substitute phallus for the microgenitomorph.
And when Tiffauges calls Bluebeard the "Spirit of Defecation and the
Anal Angel" (226), it is once more clear, as it was when we noted that
he "devours" his object choices, that the need for the substitute origi-
nates in those psychic dispositions that precede the phallic stage, with
its genital organization of the psyche.[3]

Late in the novel when Tiffauges has gained control over the boys at
Kaltenborn, he once more compares himself to Bluebeard, who has

    2. Tournier has written a short book, *Gilles et Jeanne,* that explores the relationship
between Gilles de Rais and Jeanne d'Arc.
    3. Commenting on Tiffauges in *The Wind Spirit,* Tournier claims that his character is in
fact not sexual, but "pre-sexual or proto-sexual" (98). This is true only if the oral and anal
phases of psychic development are desexualized. As Whitmont has said of the latter phase, "The
anal experience is one of power over substance and objects, assertion and control over matter,
objects or people. . . . It represents the first experience of self-will, defiance and an egotistic
power attitude. It establishes the first point of reference of a self-consciousness in the flowing
earth and 'swamp-intestinal' existence—the endless cycle of natural life and exchange of
matter" (241). Abel never leaves the swamp for the dry ground of the ego.

become "slack, sloppy, rawboned, broken-down" (332). Just as the horse comes to life only when harnessed and saddled, so, too, Tiffauges becomes himself only when "harnessed by the body of a child" (332). Only when Bluebeard or Tiffauges are ridden do they gain vitality (and virility), but that vitality is used to conscript children for the Nazi war effort. Going from village to village to claim children for the Nazis, Tiffauges is given the title of the "Ogre of Kaltenborn," thus joining the malign pantheon of ogres that includes Hitler and Goering.

The distorted image of sexuality works in the service of Thanatos, and the phallus is, finally, a *false* phallus: Bluebeard is a gelding. Abel, like his alter ego, suffers the consequences of castration—he has discovered his sexual potency *outside* of himself in the camera or in Bluebeard—and in compensation for this loss, he spins out a pathological narrative that directly connects Abel, who is in fact severely alienated from himself, with the fate of history.

If it was Nestor who first initiated Abel into the secrets of phoria, and Bluebeard who becomes the simulacrum of power for him, it is the figure of the Erl-King—privileged both by its place in the title (*Le Roi des Aulnes* in French) and its place at the conclusion of the novel—that becomes the emblem of Tiffauges's deepest self-representations. The *Erlkönig* is Abel's primary identification once he has entered Prussia, the world of the Reich and, for him, a "promised land, the land of pure essences" (180). Tiffauges, whose vocation as an ogre is to decipher signs, believes he has discovered in the black-and-white land of Prussia the perfect textual surface upon which to read his destiny, and the Erl-King becomes a crucial cipher in the record of his journey toward apocalypse.

Tiffauges encounters this figure just after its corpse has been exhumed from the peat bogs of the "hyperborean lands" of East Prussia. Gnarled and wrinkled, with leathery skin, it wore a six-pointed star of gold on a band between the eyes. Professor Keil of Königsberg, lecturing with great scholarly pomposity on the peat-bog man, argues that its presence suggests the beginnings of a "strictly Nordic and even Germanic" (188) religion that was beginning at the same time as Christianity was springing to life in the Mediterranean. The professor, speaking in the pseudo-scientific jargon of the Nazis, continues:

> I will just add that our ancestor was exhumed near here in a little wood of alders, of the black variety common to marshes. And here I can't help thinking of Goethe, the greatest poet in the German language, and the ballad of 'The Erl-King,' at once his

most famous and his most mysterious work. It sings to our German ears, it lulls our German hearts, it is the true quintessence of the German soul. (188)

The peat-bog man is then christened, with an act of unconscious and malign condensation, the "Erl-King." The tiny buried figure with its six-pointed star on a band around its head becomes emblematic of the German, and Tiffauges's, soul. And, once again, poetry and history are conflated.

The title of the poem, Tournier informs us in *The Wind Spirit,* derives from Herder's mistranslation of the Danish *Eller,* "elves," into the German *Erlen,* "elms" (French *aulnes* and English "alders"). "It is unlikely," Tournier continues,

> that Goethe would have been interested in the banal legend of the king of the elves. But his imagination was inspired by the precise and original evocation of the elm, because the elm was considered to be a dark and evil tree that flourished beside stagnant ponds. . . . The marsh elm evokes the foggy plains and dunes of north Germany, and the *Erlkönig* is the ethereal, child-loving ogre who hovers over those mournful flatlands. (*The Wind Spirit,* 97; hereafter cited as WS)

Abel identifies himself with the corpse removed from the bog, in both its spectral and its childlike aspects. The malign condensation, which Professor Keil announces with Teutonic arrogance and Tiffauges unwittingly enacts, requires that a distinction be drawn: the two separate components of the condensed image, the childlike and the spectral, must be separated into their constitutive parts. The childlike corpse, "probably of a woman," comes from the "mists of time" and wears a cap like that of a "prisoner or even a convict" (189), whereas the haunting figure in Goethe's poem becomes death, the abductor of children. Tiffauges's fate as victim and victimizer is woven between these two polarized forces that are violently conjoined in his psyche.

Tiffauges's passion for lifting children becomes a perversion demonically linked to death when the Erl-King becomes for him the "very charter of phoria" (300). The St. Christopher of legend, indeed Christ himself, who bears the sins of the world on his shoulders, is "malignly inverted" by Abel's identification with Goethe's horseman, which is preceded by many analogous identifications. Childhood, or even the past itself, is an empty and ruined psychic space for Tiffauges, who therefore incessantly attempts to fill the lack with each figure of power that comes his way. But because of the insatiability of his psychological "appetite," the attempt to feed himself leads ineluctably to the death of others. The objects with which he nourishes himself become victims of his "horse-man" persona: the Erl-King galloping through the night.

The unballasted and unbalanced nature of Tiffauges's sign system has become quite clear. The "quintessence of the German soul" (188) begins to be uncannily embodied by the Frenchman; signs, to borrow Freud's formula about repetition in "Remembering, Repeating, and Working-Through," begin to be acted out rather than remembered. Tournier most astutely explores the ways that literalized mythologies bring destruction and death: Nazi mythology creates the gas chamber; French mythology creates an illusion about the universality of a heroic resistance to the German occupation.[4] Whether or not his pathological interpretation of existence finally regains its balance at the end of the novel when he lifts the Jewish child from the death camps onto his shoulders must, for the moment, remain an open question.

Tiffauges's self-interpretation, reflected in the characters with whom he identifies, is based upon perceived similarities that too often ignore essential differences between himself and the objects of identification. For Tiffauges to believe that he literally *is* Nestor or the Erl-King is to collapse the metaphorical distinction of the "as if" into the false identification of the "I am"; it is to see as literally identified—that is, as unified—what should be kept in tension by the tropological power of the metaphor and by the tension of "likeness" rather than by a desperate resolution into "sameness." Narcissus, totalizing the world into his own image, creates his own death trap.

Tiffauges fails to make this distinction and is thus driven to create an apocalyptic semiotics that sees only a conjunction between his personal fate and the march of history, indeed between himself and the unfolding of the universe within the mind of God. In itself this does not prove the aberrant nature of Tiffauges's condition, for there have been saints, mystics, and artists who have all claimed a special relationship with the

4. See, for instance, Tournier's discussion of the French response to the German occupation in *The Wind Spirit*: "Many true freedom-fighters found themselves disgusted by the grandiose proportions assumed by the Resistance myth in the postwar years, when it was made to seem that people had signed up for Resistance duty between 1940 and 1944 as routinely as they would have signed up for military service. *Here we have a fine example of a country being carried away by a mythical reconstruction of a not very glorious period in its history*" (62; emphasis added). Tournier's ouevre as a whole is very much concerned with the relationship between, to use shorthand, "myth" and "history."

divine. But Abel's personality is marked by an increasing isolation from other human beings and, more importantly, by an almost total lack of the dimension of the personal, a necessary stage in the dialectic of symbolic awareness.

There are, for instance, a number of other figures with whom Abel claims a special bond—Rasputin, St. Christopher, Hercules Pedephorus, Bacchus, Hector, and Atlas—and in every case these are archetypal, not personal, characters. Abel is a man for whom "eternity takes the place of both relatives and progeny. Old as the world, and as immortal, I can have none but putative parents and adopted children" (4); thus he exalts himself to the status of both universal creator and universal child. Out of the psychic debris that litters the personal life-world, Abel constructs the bricolage of a world-myth that makes him a central actor in the drama of the end. The tale that he weaves in order to survive soon becomes a net that drags him relentlessly toward the recognition of his affinity with the Nazi system and, finally, toward death.

But narrative links beginnings and endings, and rather than rush toward the end, I want instead to continue to work simultaneously back to Abel's psychological origins as well as forward to the conclusion, the logical consequence and the end of his process of symbolization. The elements that bind all of Tiffauges's "object choices"—which are not really objects and not really by choice—are *la phorie,* the presence of children and violence, and the aggrandizement of psychic contents characteristic of the primary processes and the inflation of every experience to the order of myth.

Tournier, in *Die Zeit,* has remarked that the "metamorphosis of a complex into a myth" lies at the heart of the novel; my own strategy is to peel away the myth to reveal the complex and then to ask about the relation of the two as shown by the narcissistic contour of his sign system. Abel employs the process of identification to construct his exaggerated self-image: "As for me, I was already there a thousand, a hundred thousand years ago. When the earth was still only a ball of fire spinning around in a helium sky the soul that lit and made it spin was mine" (3). Instead of forming a proper object choice, one that maintains the distance between self and other as a means for being in relationship, Abel fantasizes that he has *become* the object of his unconscious choice; that is, he identifies himself with the object (which therefore loses its objectivity and its otherness). Eros, the possibility of love for another, is usurped by Tiffauges's megalomania, a state always associated with the apocalyptic fantasies of Thanatos. If Narcissus cannot be the center of the world, there should be no world.

Tiffauges, who identifies himself with both St. Christopher and the Erl-King, is an ogre who loves the raw flesh of steak tartare, whose mentor had an "appetite out of the ordinary" (20), and who symbolically devours the flesh of children around him. Although he claims to love children and to be ruled by Eros, Abel nonetheless exhibits the ambivalence characteristic of a possession by an archetypal content. Such a possession, an eruption of the collective into the personal psyche, indicates that the grandiose egotism of Tiffauges is in fact a radical absence of a functioning ego. The "lining of narcissism"—just as in Rhoda's fall toward death in *The Waves*—fails to guard against the devouring lack at the center of psychic being. Tiffauges's narcissism, his struggle with the lack, projects itself into the world, which therefore becomes not an other but only the unscrolled text of his solipsistic psyche.

Again and again, Abel reveals the "omnipotence of thought" that Freud associates with primitives, children, and the regression to infantile mentation that characterizes psychosis. We have already seen a number of examples of such omnipotent thinking; another appears when, after having established himself at Kaltenborn, Abel writes to himself that "one of the heaviest fatalities that hangs over me—or should I say one of the brightest benedictions?—is that I can't ask a question or form a wish without fate sooner of later taking it upon itself to provide an answer" (345).

Narcissism, which inevitably entails a form of apocalyptic thinking, involves just this assertion of a direct and unique connection between an individual and either the encompassing movements of history or of fate itself. A Tiffaugean form of symbol making—an incandescent absolutizing of signs that incessantly refers back to the sign maker—inevitably creates its own Armageddon. Such apocalypticism leads through its inherent logic to a "malign inversion," Tiffauges's term for what might be called a destructive transvaluation of values that produces an annihilation of meaning.

The apocalypse does not occur *at* the end of the world; it *is* the end of the world. Freud observes that "there are two mechanisms in this 'end of the world' idea: in one case, the whole libidinal cathexis is drained off to the loved object, while, in the other, it all flows back to the ego" (N, 33). Abel clearly enacts the second mechanism, but since his fragile ego structure is unable to bear such psychic weight, the contents of libidinal cathexes are reprojected upon the world.

Only at the end of a world, whether that world be that of an individual psyche or of a social group, do apocalyptic sign systems gain credence.

Or, to phrase it in the language of semiotics itself, only when a network of signs that grounds personal or cultural identity fails to secure meaning for those who use such a network, who live within such a *narrative* of existence, will there be a crisis that entails a conflict of interpretation at a level that disrupts the foundations of the individual or the collective identity. The struggle for identity occurs on the battlefield of signs; identity is constructed by a network of signifiers.

In an apocalyptic mentality such as Tiffauges's, the tensive distance between signifier and signified collapses completely. The "bar" dividing the two is abolished; the sign is literalized and absolutized; the possessor of signs becomes possessed by signs that have become autonomous powers. Tiffauges forgets—and this is a fundamental forgetting—that signs are our fallible means of probing existence and are not identical with a direct revelation of the absolute.

This collapse of the significatory space is, from one point of view, a collapse into purely mythical consciousness, about which Cassirer writes that "the word which denotes [the] thought content is not a mere conventional symbol, but is merged with its object in an indissoluble unity. The conscious experience is not merely wedded to the word, but is consumed by it" (58). His life is, from within his perspective, the enactment not of a personal myth or of a collective matrix of myth, but of the world-myth itself. A megalomania, which shows a *failure* to establish a stable self in the world, is the logical end of Abel's sign making; and true to the circle of semiosis and pathology, his sign making is the logical result of his megalomania.

Tiffauges is completely without the ballast provided by the presence of otherness. To ballast is to stabilize, but what is it that stabilizes a system of symbols such as the one that Tiffauges's, a product of his time and of his own pathology, has created? We have already encountered one clue to what might indicate where the boundary to absolute narcissism is crossed: the interpreter's stance toward the relationship between signifier and signified. Tiffauges is an apocalyptic reader of signs who draws the entire universe, without remainder, into his symbolic constructions. All of us at times exhibit this tendency, for we want, in perhaps the fundamental *wish* of human life, the world to be a mirror for ourselves.

If an attempt like Tiffauges's succeeds, however, the otherness of the other is destroyed, and everything becomes subsumed in a self-reflexive script. Such apparent omnipotence, which is actually utter powerlessness, necessitates that the self be envisioned as a prison-house without any "outside." Without any possibility of the existence of an other, which by remaining outside of the apocalyptic economy of narcissism can offer a hope of transformation, the subject will inevitably implode into its primitive components.

Tiffauges does retain an inchoate sense of otherness, though it is constantly threatened and often overcome by his narcissistic inclinations. He begins his ruminations by accepting Rachel's naming of him as a monster, for, as he says, "if you don't want to be a monster, you've got to be like your fellow creatures, in conformity with the species, the image of our relations" (4). Abel implies that beneath the superficial oppositions we are all monsters—much like Freud's belief that we are all neurotic, or that the way to the "normal" is through an examination of the "grotesque"—and that the only real choice is whether our monstrosity will conform with that of our fellows or whether we will construct a monstrous form of our own. Tiffauges chooses the latter alternative, which, although dangerous because it immediately and radically marginalizes him, is also able to give him a moral perspective on the monstrous society in which he finds himself.

Abel curses the new government of 1938 as a "rogues' gallery" led by the inept Albert LeBrun. He knows that "war, an absolute evil, is inevitably the object of a satanic cult. It is a black mass celebrated in broad daylight by Mammon, and the blood-bolstered idols before which the duped masses are made to kneel are called Country, Sacrifice, Heroism and Honor" (74). He writes, with an incisive awareness, that "Love, while advocated in the abstract, is fiercely persecuted as soon as it takes on concrete form and calls itself sexuality or eroticism" (75).

Although he is tremendously fascinated with the event, Abel also protests against the execution of Weidmann, a murderer, partially as a defensive reaction to his own unconscious desire for violence, but also as a pointed attack on the hypocrisy of the legal system. Finally, he recognizes that conventional signs are "abstract, futile, and without any fateful significance" (134). Without the ballast of a common cultural foundation of meaning, Tiffauges has nowhere to turn but to his own fragmented psyche.

At points such as these, as well as when Tiffauges recognizes that he is in desperate need of deliverance and dreams of "an awakening, a break that will set me free and let me be myself" (64), he retains a degree of rationality marked by an interaction between primary and secondary processes, between signified and signifier. Consciousness of need and an ability to identify and resist the machinations of society's semiotics of death—both of which depend on at least a dormant sense of otherness—are some of the facets that establish a sense of ballast for Tiffauges's pathological predilections.

This ballast, however, erodes as the novel progresses and Tiffauges loses his capacity for discernment. Instead of recognizing the immorality of Hermann Goering, the master of the hunt, he sees only a master of scatological interpretation. He is bewildered by a woman's refusal to sew the hair of the boys at Kaltenborn into a cloak (at a time when the hair of Jews was being collected in the death camps) and remains unaware of the implications of his possession by the ghost of the Erl-King. As his narcissistic regression deepens and his omnipotent thinking increases, Tiffauges begins to lose touch with the objectivity of the world. His attitude toward purity clearly reveals this shift.

At the stage in which his moral acuity, which depends upon making distinctions, is still functional, Abel declares that "purity is the malign inversion of innocence . . . [it] is a horror of life, hatred of man, morbid passion for the void. . . . A man hagridden by the demon of purity sows ruin and death around him" (75). And yet, later in the novel, Abel himself declares that he wants to read the "pure essences" to be found in Prussia. Insofar as he wishes to read an absolutely pure language of hieroglyphs and signs that are directed solely at him, Abel has crossed the boundary into the self-referential and enclosed world of insanity, a realm in which any relationship to the other is radically attenuated, if not altogether obliterated.

The metaphorical tension between Abel's self-reflexive script and the historical dimension disappears, and he "falls" into the primary processes, of which Otto Fenichel says, "The object and the idea of the object, the object and a picture or model of the object, the object and a part of the object are equated; *similarities are not distinguished from identities; ego and nonego are not yet separated*" (47; emphasis added).

Such a collapse is made visible in Abel's identifications with the figures of myth, legend, and history, and I have noted his regression toward primary-process language. When the symbol is literalized and taken for the reality, it loses its meaning as symbol and becomes simply part of the univocal discourse of madness. The referent of all signs becomes the self, or, more accurately, a fragment of the self that has failed to develop beyond an original primary narcissism.

This partial self, folded inside out by the act of projecting its contents upon the world, reveals itself only as the discourse of others. In Tiffauges's case, the voices that mime alterity consist of absent parents, of archetypal heroes, and, finally, of the cultural symbolism of the Reich.

Although he is persistently threatened by the dissolution of the boundaries of his ego, Tiffauges, by writing and by seeking signs that will
release him from his psychological and historical devastation, struggles
against the terrible gravitational pull of his narcissism. And reality itself,
that which we are unable to assimilate and master by our sign making,
also resists his pathological assault. Freud remarks in his analysis of Dora
that "the barrier erected by repression can fall before the onslaught of a
violent emotional excitement produced by a real cause; it is possible for
a neurosis to be overcome by reality" ("Fragment," 132). Our fantastic
constructs can be deconstructed by the overwhelming force of the real,
the otherness that cannot be appropriated by the psyche through the
means of identification. In several instances, this is precisely what happens to Tiffauges.

In the context of a textual model of subjectivity, "reality" can be translated into the lexicon of narrativity: the pathological fantasies can be
overcome by other organizations of fantasy, by a narrative more powerful
than the one deformed by the repressed contents of the unconscious.
Each of these forms of alterity, the intrusion of the objective other and the
presence of a transformative narrative, appears as Tiffauges's private domain of boys nears its destruction at the hands of the Russian army. Reality
testing, to use Freud's rather ambiguous term, provides the essential ballast for symbolic constructions.

At times, sheer reality devastates Tiffauges's penchant for making
signs; it defeats his powers of interpretation. For example, when the
Prussian peasants are fleeing before the onslaught of the Russian army,
Tiffauges spots a corpse that, now barely recognizable as human, had
been run over time and again by trucks and carts. This sight, for Abel,
bears no "symbolic aura" but belongs to the "most naked horror" (338).

The horror of the real defies any transposition by even apocalyptic
semiotics; its power resists being absorbed into Tiffauges's myopic
world. A similar response occurs when the boys of Kaltenborn celebrate
the summer solstice. "This time," says Tiffauges, "there is no need for
interpretation or for any deciphering grid. This ceremony, obstinately
mingling the future and death, and throwing the boys one after the other
into the live coals, is the clear evocation, the diabolic invocation, of the
massacre of the innocents toward which we march, singing" (284).

Reality is otherness that always stands on the threshold of our interpretations (and this otherness arrives as both gift and threat). Tiffauges had
long known that "the wall of our blindness and deafness can be pene-
trated only if signs make a repeated assault on it" (102), but his sign
system had become a closed fortress whose meaning had reference only

to himself. As Lacan has said, "The formation of the *I* is symbolized in dreams by a fortress, or a stadium—its inner arena and enclosure, surrounded by marshes and rubbish-tips" (E, 5). For Tiffauges, Kaltenborn is a symbolic wall of self-referentiality whose foundation is already sinking into the surrounding swampland.

Only by the intrusion of the horror of the real and by the narratives of more percipient readers of signs, such as Ephraim the Star-Bearer or the General Count Herbert von Kaltenborn, the old Prussian who had been commandant of the fortress before its conscription by the Nazis, can Tiffauges take a step toward the liberation that will free him from the malign influence of his semiomachia. The general, an antithetical balance to Nestor, teaches Tiffauges not just the alpha and the omega, but the ways in which signs can be inverted and made demonic.

After sketching the differences between weak symbols and strong ones, the general then warns Tiffauges about the dangers of being a reader and writer of signs:

> Signs are irritable, and the symbol thwarted becomes a diabol. . . .
> For there is a terrifying moment when the sign no longer accepts being carried by a creature as a standard is carried by a soldier. . . .
> When the symbol devours the thing symbolized, when the cross-bearer becomes the crucified, when a malign inversion overthrows phoria, then the end of the world is at hand. Symbol, no longer ballasted by anything, becomes master of heaven. It proliferates, insinuates itself everywhere, and shatters into a thousand meanings that don't mean anything any more. (303)

"Symbol, no longer ballasted by anything" is, in French, "Le symbole n'etant plus leste par rien." "Lester" means "ballast," but in its most familiar form, "[se] lester" refers to eating, to filling oneself with food.[5] When we are not well fed, when the hunger of the libido runs rampant— as in the never-fulfilled, always-lacking psyche of Abel the Ogre—then violence becomes the only recourse in the search for nourishment.

Symbols are not neutral terms of description; they have power. This power, though it can never completely read the rune of the world, can help keep us moving on the track of interpretation. But when the symbol loses its ballast and becomes the diabol, the power of the symbolic becomes destructive and ruins, either by its pathological misappropria-

---

5. My thanks to David Price for this observation, as well as for his extremely helpful critique of earlier versions of this chapter.

tion or by its loss of trust in the meaning of signs, those under its
influence. And though Tiffauges does catch a glimpse of the infernal
inversion of signs to which he had long ago unconsciously consented,
the force of those signs churns relentlessly on, indifferently crushing
him, Ephraim, the boys at Kaltenborn, and the Nazis.

The commandant, who knows and lives within a traditional system of
signs, is someone who can read the true import of the Nazis: "The truth
is that ever since it began the Third Reich has been the product of
symbols, which have taken over control. The inflation of 1923 was an
eloquent warning, though no one understood it: that cloud of worthless
bank notes, monetary symbols symbolizing nothing" (304). In his last
conversation with the Frenchman, the commandant speaks propheti-
cally, telling Tiffauges that he doesn't yet see "what this awful prolifera-
tion of symbols leads to. In the sign-saturated sky a storm is gathering
which will be violent as an apocalypse, and which will engulf us all!"
(306).

The commandant's interpretation offers Tiffauges a moment in which
he might reinterpret his own symbolic productions, in which he might
begin to write a new identity for himself. And yet, even after the exegesis
of the operations of the symbol and the diabol, Tiffauges is "haunted by
the image of the Erl-King" (339), and death exerts an even more compul-
sive fascination on him. He sits in an all-night vigil with the decapitated
body of one of the boys at Kaltenborn and then makes a confession in his
notebook: "I keep pushing away a suspicion that haunts me so insistently
I'm going to let it write itself down on this page in the secrecy of the
night. Could it be that my vigil by Hellmut's body has given me forever a
taste for a flesh more grave, more marmoreal than that which is snorting
and snoring sweetly in the hypnodrome?" (345). His suspicion is that the
dead body nourishes the ogre even more than the live one, a suspicion
that seems to be confirmed when he is covered by a cyclone of blood
from another body in a "ferocious baptism" that attests to his "dignity as
Erl-King" (347).

It is only after these events, however, that Tiffauges discovers Ephraim, the Jewish child from Auschwitz, and helps to keep the boy alive.
Beginning where the old count left off, Ephraim tells Tiffauges a narrative that explains the true significance of those symbols—Canada, a
woman's hair, a roll call at Kaltenborn—that Tiffauges had assumed to be
directed at him but that were from the beginning, unknown to him,
already malign inversions of the actions of the Nazis. It is the third-
person narrator who reports the result of these conversations: "Thus,
through Ephraim's long confession, Tiffauges, steeped in horror, saw an

infernal city remorselessly building up which corresponded stone by stone to the phoric city he himself had dreamed of at Kaltenborn . . . all his inventions, all his discoveries were reflected in the horrible mirror, inverted and raised to hellish incandescence" (357). But the moment of recognition does not, as we might expect, lead to a reversal of Tiffauges's entrenched narcissism. With the Russian troops already inside the fortress of Kaltenborn and Tiffauges's self-styled domain burning as if it were the day of the Great Tribulation, "it was the peaceful and disincarnate face of the Erl-King, wrapped in his shroud of peat, which presented itself to his mind as the ultimate resource, the ultimate retreat" (367). This, then, is the image lodged most deeply in Tiffauges's psyche: the ghostly figure, wrapped in his shroud of death.

Soon after the moment in which the image floats into his mind, Tiffauges lifts Ephraim onto his shoulders: the child-bearer carries the astrophore. Having lost his glasses, Abel allows Ephraim to guide him into the black alders of the marshes, into the bog of the Erl-King—to the archaic past of the unconscious and the self-annihilation for which Tiffauges had for so long yearned. Drawn toward the final conflation of Goethe's horseman and the peat-bog man, Abel becomes the "Steed of Israel," guided by Ephraim's hands. But isn't Abel's animal self still named Bluebeard?

In its final scene, the novel leaves us with Tiffauges sinking into the bog and looking back up at a six-pointed star wheeling in the heavens. It concludes with an image in which opposites—life and death, the earth and the heavens, the Erl-King and the astrophore—are held together, but held together only as they disappear beneath the dark mud of the swamp or into the blankness of the white page after the last word has been written. Many critics see the novel's ending as a moment of redemption, but I read it only as the logical and fatal result of the entire course of Abel's (and the Nazis') delusional construction of an absolutely self-referential world.[6]

The viscous swamp receives its own: Tiffauges's "viscous self," of which he had written that "it's a heavy, rancorous, moody self, always weltering in tears and semen, obstinately attached to its habits and its past. . . . I carry it deep inside me like a wound, this innocent and tender being, slightly deaf, slightly shortsighted, so easily taken in, so slow to

6. According to Susan Petit's well-argued account, the novel concludes with "redemption, for at the end of the book Tiffauges is redeemed by his sacrifice of himself in an attempt to save Ephraim from the invading Russians." Though it is a vexed issue, I continue to read the ending differently. The malign conversion of the history of his personal psyche and a collective history he cannot truly comprehend act to tear Tiffauges apart. The eater is eaten.

muster itself up against misfortune" (21). The wounded self, attempting to heal itself by making the world its slave and its salvific theater, ends only by constructing an infernal narcissistic drama with only one actor.

The end has come and we, as readers—as creators of semiotic reconstructions—are left only with our interpretive predilections, pathological and otherwise, and a welter of signs we must shape into a meaningful text. Is it possible for us to avoid Abel's narcissistic semiotic, which, in the end, presses toward a self-enclosed text of madness? How might we heed J. J. White's succinct dictum reminding us that "the man who reads too much into what he sees is in fact blind" (242)? Or are we as fated as Tiffauges to fill our pages with self-generated signs that fill the gaps within our own psyches?

The Ogre raises the fierce question of the relationship between psyche and sign; and, even more emphatically, it demonstrates the consequences of a narcissistic symbolization unballasted by the presence within the symbolic of others. Failing to pass through the cut of castration from the mirror stage to the stage of the symbol, Tiffauges remains embedded in the world of mirroring identifications rather than progressing into the world of dialogue.

His career, leading from a garage on the outskirts of Paris to a moor in the flatlands of Prussia, suggests that without "ballast," a force that acts to balance the inherent egocentricity of our interpretations, we are bound to fall into the mire constructed by our narcissistic symbolic activity. Only by remaining open to the presence of the other, to others' readings of our own self-constructed narrative about ourselves, and to the necessity of the significatory gap that marks the presence of metaphor will we possibly be able to avoid the narcissistic semiotics, and the concommitant fate, of the Ogre of Kaltenborn.

6

Rewriting Narcissus:
Art and the Self in *Daniel Martin*

Mr. Specula Speculans had not been quite fair: a love of mirrors may appear to be only too literally *prima facie* evidence
of narcissism, but it can also be symbolic of an attempt to see
oneself as others see one—to escape the first person, and
become one's own third.

—John Fowles

John Fowles's novel *Daniel Mar-
tin,* like *The Waves* and *The Ogre,* concerns itself with narcissism and its
consequences. But whereas Abel Tiffauges's condition is inescapable and
leads inevitably toward his death in the swamp, Daniel Martin, who is
both the novel's protagonist as well as its "author," suggests a way out of
the narcissistic enclosure ruled by Thanatos. In fact, Martin responds to
his crisis in the same way as Tiffauges: he writes. But the act of writing
his text, which is a creation of himself—for we can know no other
"Daniel Martin" than *Daniel Martin*[1]—is not only a pathological spinning out of a narcissistic semiotic, but also an act of liberation, although
it, too, must face death and the ruins at the "end of the world."

The novel, which plays incessantly with tense and voice, begins with a
harvest scene from Daniel's boyhood Devon in August of 1942. The son
of the local vicar, Dan helps the farmhands with the harvest and afterwards carves his initials in a beech tree: "Deep incisions in the bark,
peeling the gray skin away to the sappy green of the living stem" (9). The

---

1. For a discussion of other such fictional "self-begettings," see Steven Kellman's *Self-
Begetting Novel.*

beech is his first writing parchment, and the beech is a book, a word
cognate to Middle English *book, boke, bok;* Anglo-Saxon *boc,* a writing,
record, book; from *boc, bece,* a beech writing material of the Teutonic
nations. The beech is a primitive book, unknown as such to Dan, who, by
marking the tree with the incisions of time, already memorializes himself
in writing. To do so, he must peel the old skin away and reach for a green
core, still alive and growing. The novel as a whole takes the same path: to
remember and write, to write as a form of remembrance, is to reach
toward the green core of the self.[2]

The adult Daniel, we soon learn, is a successful but discontented
middle-aged scriptwriter living in Los Angeles and having an affair with a
young Scottish actress, Jenny McNeill. Unexpectedly he is called home
to Oxford by his ex-wife, Nell; her twin sister, Jane; and his old university
friend, Anthony, a philosophy don who is Jane's husband and is now
dying of cancer.

During their university days, the four had formed a close quartet: Dan
was a budding playwright; the "Heavenly Twins" were rising actresses;
and Anthony was on the road to an appointment in philosophy. Most
importantly for the later course of their lives (and Dan's eventual decision to turn to the genre of the novel), Dan and Jane, after accidentally
finding a woman's dead and rotting body in the reeds of the river, had
shared a single *acte gratuit* of lovemaking just before graduation (and
Dan's marriage to Nell, Jane's to Anthony).

That day, which became known in Dan's private mythology as that of
the "woman in the reeds," forms a nexus in the novel: it is death and the
stench of decay; a prelude, catalyst, and accompaniment for love; an
image of Dan's mother (dead since he was four); and an emblem for all
the lost possibilities entailed by finitude and mortality. The woman in the
reeds is the always-lost object that Daniel has compulsively, and unsuc-
cessfully, attempted to recapture throughout his adult life and the central absence to which his novel, at its deepest levels a creation of a new
self through the complexities of writing, must be addressed.

What holds true for psychic activity holds true as well for the more
specialized activity of the novelist, for, as Robert Alter reminds us, "the
objects of representation of all novels are necessarily recollected objects, or to be more precise, recollected-and-reinvented objects" (154).
As Daniel remarks later in the novel, "You create out of what you lack"
(268); it is the emptiness at the heart of the self, a void connected to

2. Fowles, an avid naturalist, writes in *The Tree* that writing, or reading, a novel is like
walking through a forest. One never knows ahead of time which turn to take.

both a Lacanian lack and a Heideggerian reading of nothingness, that allows the interior space and motivation for creativity.

Martin returns to England and is reconciled with Anthony, who asks that he make an attempt to "retrieve" Jane from depression and a bitterness that had accrued throughout the years of their marriage, primarily from her unwillingness to live out her most genuine talents (acting and a passion for Daniel). Jane is, in fact, something like the beech tree in Devon and like Martin himself: she is covered by dead layers of bark and must somehow be stripped down to a level where vitality still runs green. Anthony, having received Dan's consent to do what he can to help Jane, jumps from his hospital window to his death, leaving Jane and Daniel alone to cut a path toward each other, to retrieve the lost possibility that was enacted only during the day of the *acte gratuit.*

If one of the major aspects of narcissism is, as Ovid says of his character, a "hard pride" and an inability or unwillingness to love the other, then both Dan and Jane are offered the possibility of overcoming their respective forms of narcissism. The course of *Daniel Martin,* for both of the characters, is from a privatized and self-absorbed world toward a public world shared with others.

In addition to their gradual and somewhat grudging recovery of one another, Jane's main instrument of self-liberation is politics—she gives books by Antonio Gramsci and by Georg Lukács to Daniel—and Daniel's is literature, the composition of a novel, a form "that would tally better with the real structure of [his] racial being and mind... something dense, interweaving, treating time as horizontal, like a skyline; not cramped, linear and progressive" (331). It is only the mythic time of fiction that will allow Martin to gain access to his lost self; psychic recovery is enacted as textual creation. Fowles himself has declared that "narcissism, or pygmalionism, is the essential vice a writer must have" ("Notes," 162), and Daniel Martin declares that "every artist lives in an equivalent of my old Oxford room, with its countless mirrors" (275).

It is a cliché to claim that the artist is the narcissist par excellence, who nonetheless deserves the tolerance of lesser individuals, and *Daniel Martin* is a critique of this position. While the novel admits a narcissistic aspect for both capitalist society and the artist, it also struggles with ways to heal the wound of self-absorption. Art, as Fowles-Martin demonstrates, is a form of narcissism that has the paradoxical power of overcoming narcissism.

Socially, Martin identifies the essential problem of his generation as "overweening narcissism" (593), the fact that "all that my generation and the one it sired have ever cared a damn about is personal destiny; all the other destinies have become blinds" (157). And he sees this self-obsession manifested in television and the cinema, which have "atrophied a vital psychic function: the ability to imagine for oneself" (274). If the artist is one who lives in the imagination, it is primarily a personal, or personally appropriated, field of images, one that the artist is called upon to craft and that, in turn, crafts the artist. The narcissist (what might in this context be called a "false" narcissist), on the other hand, is captured by the images of others through television, movies, advertising, political propaganda, the voice of authority in whatever guise.

In making the move from screenwriter to novelist, Martin is recovering his more personal and authentic imagination. Through an imagination activated through writing, he is reclaiming the "real history" (15) of who he is. But since "real history"—as the psychoanalysts have confirmed—always and inevitably involves memory, fantasy, narrativity, and illusion, the only possibility of authenticity lies in reordering the story through another more encompassing story that leads us beyond the room of mirrors.

The self is not an object, a preformed given that may be comprehended and grasped; it is, rather, an enacted performance that must be written and rewritten, blocked and rehearsed, over and over again until the play ceases its run. It is also a performance that requires others: directors, players in the troupe, a technical crew, and an audience. Subjectivity, the ongoing revisioning of the self, is a political act, or, to echo my previous discussion of psychoanalysis, one in which object relations have an essential role.

Jane provides Dan, the disillusioned and politically unattached intellectual, with the incentives and ideas that lead him to think more deeply about the role of politics in relation to both life and art. She introduces him to Gramsci's philosophy of praxis and to Lukács's thinking on critical realism. Bruce Woodcock has argued that in *Daniel Martin* "the relationship between politics and art manifests itself in Fowles's choice to abandon the realms of fantasy for a more Lukácsian model of the novel, to assert the novel as what he calls a 'humanistic enterprise'" (144). This, in part, provides Dan with the justification for writing a "realistic" novel, part of which is to choose his "real" self for the protagonist rather than an "invented" stand-in who might display the more fashionable attributes of existential angst and pessimism about the hopes for modern humanity.

But such a focus on a realism that is a form of "anti-fantasy" must, of course, be taken with a large grain of appreciation for the conjuring that is going on in the text.[3] The choice of a "real" self is that of an already-"invented" character concocted by that ghostwriter, John Fowles. And although the novel in many ways does follow the traditions of realism that Lukács championed over Ernst Bloch's defense of the experimental modernism of Kafka and others, Fowles is also an old hand at playing the compositional magus.

Daniel Martin shifts tense and voice, it collates texts "by" both Martin and Jenny McNeill, and it even goes so far as to allow McNeill to speak as a character to her inventor in the form of his alterego, Daniel Martin: "She turned in front of him, mimicking a niece at the end of a treat. A smile, a look into his eyes. 'Thank you for having me. In all senses. And I think the rewrite of this scene's been so much better than the first draft' " (627).

All of these are narrative devices by which the novel revels in its own artifice—the hallmark of the self-reflexive, narcissistic novel from Apuleius and Cervantes down through Nabokov and Pynchon—with great abandon at every troping turn. It is important, however, to take seriously Martin's (and Fowles's) claims for realism, for Fowles uses his panoply of narrative tricks in order metaphorically to mime his experience of the world, that labyrinth in which truth and illusion flicker incessantly through one another. He is, in fact, engaged in a critique of political conservatism (especially in the sections on Hollywood and on Fenwick, the Tory member of Parliament) as well as a tropological exploration of art and selfhood.

Just as significant as the various tricks in which Fowles reveals the fictionality of his fiction is the stated telos of the novel: "It is not finally a matter of skill, of knowledge, of intellect; of good luck or bad; but of choosing and learning to feel" (629). It is not only the novel as a complex narrative structure that draws us into its signifying web, but also the novel as a contemplation on the place of emotion in human affairs, the attempt to peel back dead layers until the green core is reached.

It is just this green core of the self that is at stake when Martin begins

3.   The same can be said of Michel Tournier. He, too, not only in *The Ogre* but also in *Gemini* and elsewhere knows the tricks of his trade, the means of showing fictionality as he simultaneously deals with the business of mimesis. About *The Ogre,* he explains that his "aim was to achieve a realism that became fantastic only through an extreme of precision and rationalism: hyperrealism plus hyperrationalism." In a more general vein, Tournier's intention with his fiction is to "avoid formal innovation, to use only the most traditional, conservative, and reassuring of forms, but to fill them with a content having none of those qualities" (WS, 93, 162). Such content, however, necessarily changes the form of narration as well.

to write his novel and to rewrite his life. During his tenure at Oxford, Dan's room reflected the state of being of its occupant:

> The most striking effect was of a highly evolved (if not painfully out-of-hand) narcissism, since the room had at least fifteen mirrors on its wall. True, they had been collected for their Art Nouveau frames, or at least allegedly; but no other room in Oxford can have provided such easy access to the physical contemplation of self. . . . There had been a list of "characters" in the manner of La Bruyere. Daniel was dubbed Mr. Specula Speculans "who died of shock on accidentally looking into a mirror without its glass and thereby discovering a true figure of his talents in place of the exquisite lineaments of his face." (52)

Martin is the man who gazes into mirrors, who is able to place himself in a position of both observer and participant. At Oxford, Martin is enthralled by "physical contemplation" in the literal mirrors, while the novel that he composes to mirror his "real self" is a construction of "true figures" that reflect psychically and imaginally, not literally.

The true self is a field of symbols, ever changing, and to be perceived it needs a mode of perception other than the fixed, glassy-eyed stare of Narcissus. Whereas earlier in his life the mirrors were used to reflect the self, by the time he writes his novel, the self itself has gained a certain reflective shine and is used by the author not only as a means toward self-definition but also to reflect upon the world as a whole.

Even in his description of his past undergraduate self, Martin intimates the way art and the self riddle the space of each other. The mirrors are contained in Art Nouveau frames that, "against a background of austerity, rationing, and universal conformity" (52), have an intrinsic worth of their own for Martin. Already, art provides the framing context for his self-reflections. Undoubtedly, one mirror's image reflects off of others in the room, creating multiple perspectives on Martin, all of which are real and all of which are illusions.

The centrality of reflection to art is reinforced by the fact that Barney Dillon, in an act of undergraduate wit, gives Martin the moniker Mr. Specula Speculans. But even from his Oxford days, the mirroring of the mirrors was related to the play of art. As I will show at more length in a moment, Martin consistently sees himself and his world as parts of an art object: a play, a painting, a poem, a novel. This is not merely the clever allusional prattle of a writer, but a comprehensive metaphor for human existence, the metaphor of existence as a text and of the self as a figural composition.

The Oxford journalist lampooned Martin with the accusatory jest that the latter only saw his true face when the glass was removed, when he gazed on a nonreflective emptiness. I take this in several senses: first, as the way the statement was obviously intended—as a barb to puncture artistic and social pretensions. Second—and here I move immediately beyond the context of the passage and push through a host of associations to see what else might be heard, though not explicitly said—as a truth about the void at the core of the human self, about the non-reflective "tain" of the mirror discussed by Derrida (*Dissemination,* 33) and explicated further by Rodolphe Gasché.

Third, to return to the more prosaic content of the novel, the gibe speaks about Martin's narcissistic character, for the narcissist often does experience himself as empty, a void that must be filled with images reflected from others so that the masquerade of identity can continue. In order to lay the groundwork for a further discussion of the self as an art object—or, better, as an artistic process—Martin's narcissistic position must first be outlined, for this narcissism is an inextricable strand of his artistic vision.

As he stands with Jane in Egypt—they are ostensibly there for him to research a script on General Kitchener—Martin briefly wonders whether he really wants to resolve his relationship with her. Any such resolution would entail a surrender of his quest for other women, as well as a shift in his relationship with his own "childhood self, permanently unforgiving of its deprivations" (556). To write means to acknowledge that the deprivations, the scars of the early battles of narcissism and ego-formation, are ineradicably a part of the psyche and cannot be willfully cast off.

The young child requires what Alice Miller, following Margaret Mahler and remaining within the myth, calls "mirroring" or "echoing." "If a child is lucky enough," she writes, "to grow up with a mirroring mother, who allows herself to be cathected narcissistically, who is at the child's disposal . . . then a healthy self-feeling can gradually develop in the growing child" (32). The mother provides the mirroring environment, one that echoes the child's independent but needy being, that is requisite for a healthy passage of normal narcissistic development.[4]

4. While Miller, like most psychoanalytic theorists, concentrates solely on the role of the mother in the process of maturation, Fowles seems to have felt this lack, this psychological absence, on the part of his father as well. I am not aware of any direct comments about his mother, but the obsession with the "unattainable" versus the "real" woman—the goddess

It is unclear what kind of mothering, fictional though it must have been, that Martin enjoyed or was denied. He writes in the chapter entitled "The Umbrella" that "my mother died just before my fourth birthday, and I really cannot remember her at all; only the dimmest ghost of a bed surmounted by a tired brown face" (75). The "ghost" is perhaps the most frequently used image in Martin's novel of himself, and it is certainly an image that provides a key to his private mythology, his public figures, and his need to write, "an exorcism by the written word" (253).

The ghost here, curiously, is of the bed rather than the mother, but this is merely displaced affect, for it is actually the lost mother who haunts and unconsciously determines Martin's itinerant passage from true to false self, from woman to woman, from mirror to mirror, from the Oxford stage to the silver screen (which, as it shines in the dark movie halls, both reflects and obscures the audience).

Martin himself, now in the third person and watching himself from a distance, comments about his predilections:

> He was arguably not even looking for women in all this, but collecting mirrors still: surfaces before which he could make himself naked—or at any rate more naked than he could before other men—and see himself reflected. A psychoanalyst might say he was searching for the lost two-in-one identity of his first months of life; some solution for his double separation trauma, the universal one of infancy and the private experience of literally losing his mother. (239)

Indeed. And Fowles, speaking in a more mimetically autobiographical mode, has clarified this sense even more: "Imaginatively, it is the lost ones who count, firstly because they stand so perfectly for the original lost woman and secondly (but perhaps no less importantly) because they are a prime source of fantasy and of guidance, like Ariadne with her thread, in the labyrinth of his other worlds" ("Hardy and the Hag," 40).

Loss leads directly into the realms of fantasy and myth: as compensation, to be sure, but also as an imaginal re-creation that by taking the loss into itself, by returning time and again to the tear that marks the place of loss—the castration complex of psychoanalysis—is able to convert the loss into an artistic creation. Inscribing the psychic loss as

---

versus the human partner—in his novels points toward a deep sense of loss and an equally deep attempt to recover that which has been lost. He does, of course, attest to the importance of this process for the creation of his fiction.

a literary text, the text retains the loss—this is part of what we learn from deconstruction—but also opens the way for the response of communities of interpretation and acts as a reminder, one which paradoxically has a healing quality, of the loss we have all suffered. Writing is a kind of unending *Aufhebung*—recapitulating and overcoming—of wound, loss, and fragmentation.

And a part of this elevation, this reconstellation of elements at a "higher" place of consciousness, involves memory, which, as Mnemosyne, gives birth to the arts. The last sentence of the chapter prior to "The Umbrella," which deals with Martin's decision to return to England and his unresolved past, reads as follows: "I was not really flying to New York, and home; but into an empty space" (74). This, once again, is the emptiness of the unconscious, the emptiness the narcissist yearns to evade forever, and the emptiness that evokes and resists Martin's imaginative labor. The novelistic stage is set for an encounter with Nell, Anthony, and Jane, but the ghost of the mother necessarily intervenes, appears uncannily and immediately once the process of remembering is given consent.

But even before the mother's death is related, an epigraph taken from George Seferis's poem "Man" announces memory as the theme of the chapter: "What can a flame remember? If it remembers a little less than is necessary, it goes out; if it remembers a little more than is necessary, it goes out. If only it could teach us, while it burns, to remember correctly" (75). Martin is setting out on a voyage of remembrance—Proust echoes close by—and undertaking his own anamnesis that will, he hopes, unearth the ghosts of the unconscious in order to, at last, bury them properly.

And yet he says, "I really cannot remember her at all" (75). What, then, does he choose to remember in her place? Who fills the space of the lost one? First, Aunt Millie, a simple-minded relative who acts as a substitute mother for Martin (and whom he reads through Flaubert's *Un Coeur Simple*); next, the father, always carrying his black umbrella; and finally Nancy Reed, who initiates Martin into the mysteries of sexuality. The latter pair is most important.

Daniel's father, "whose real fear was of any nakedness of feeling" and whose "real faith was in order" (78), had only one real passion, and that was for gardening. Because he could not always get the rare shrubs he wanted, the vicar would now and again steal cuttings or seeds and hide them in the umbrella that he carried with him regardless of the weather. In addition to his love of plants, Daniel's father gave him "other poetries" (80), such as a copy of the 1820 anthology of Bewick's work "patched together round Gay's *Fables*" (81), the most fascinating of which were of

a dog pissing on a cleric's gown and of the sleeping man surrounded by
two women, one clothed and one not.

The other poetry, literally this time, was the first volume of Robert
Herrick's *Hesperides,* with its "mingled brutality and eroticism" and "un-
derlying pagan humanity" (82). With both Bewick and Herrick, Martin
clearly recognizes the father's function of censoring—Lacan's *non*-du-
pere—but is also willing to detour around the censor, to learn secrecy
and the art of hiding, of "rearranging the books so that no empty space
showed" (82), so that he could obtain knowledge and enjoy pleasure.
And, to state the obvious, it is art, pictorial and verbal, that gives access
to the erotic and to self-discovery—and it is no accident, in the logic of
the novel, that Martin becomes an artist himself.

But art is not alone, and not even primary, in its capacity to engender
pleasure and discovery. The first person with whom Martin shares sexual
pleasure is a farm girl named Nancy Reed, whose family owned Thorncombe (which later becomes his retreat) when he was a boy. In the
chapter under discussion, Nancy first appears; an image of her in church
moves through Dan's mind as he walks along the road carrying, against
his will, his father's umbrella.

It is only much later in the novel, after the loosening of the relationship with Jenny and the concomitant reunion with Jane has progressed
much further along, that we get the full story of his adolescent sexual
initiations with Nancy. When finally they kiss each other, "her lips tasted
of thyme and caraway seeds, her body was his lost mother's, her giving
forgave in a few seconds all he had thought he could never forgive"
(358). The mother, in the retrospecular memory of the author, is regained in Nancy, who in turn becomes for him a "crystal that preformed"
(575) all of Martin's other relationships with women, for the temporarily
regained object never stops being the always elusive object as well. The
fort and the *da* of Freud's grandson's game and of signification as a whole
are inseparable.

By the time Martin goes up to Oxford, all the elements that will create
the narcissistic need for a mirror-filled room—a roomful of reflections
and mirages—are in place: the lost mother; the distant father; sexual
initiation as a sense of *re*discovery; and the implicated, folded-together
experiences of loss, the erotic, and art. The father's black umbrella, full
of stolen seed, becomes, first, Dan's penis spilling its semen with Nancy,
and then the pen that writes—in Thorncombe's "library" that once was
Nancy's bedroom—the textual recovery of the past that leads the way
toward a fertile future for Dan and Jane as well as for readers of *Daniel
Martin.*

If his narcissism, as well as that of his generation, is to be overcome, it will require a work of narrative art that enacts the conviction that the self itself is an artwork. By writing himself, Martin believes he can re-write the deepest patterns at work in his life. Throughout the entire novel, we see Martin envisioning himself and those close to him as if they were part of an artistic process, characters in a play. The self becomes textualized, a composition of tropes.

At the simplest level, this is seen in the way the characters view their life situations as analogous to artists or works of art. The novel's opening chapter, "The Harvest," is compared by Martin to a Brueghel (with Auden's "Musée des Beaux Arts" another close intertextual reference); the *acte gratuit* between Jane and Dan is, in part, felt as an enactment of Rabelais's *fais ce que voudras;* Jane's affair with a professor and friendship with his ex-wife is "one of those Iris Murdoch situations" (204), a reference whereby Fowles makes a nod to his English contemporary.

Dan feels "locked up inside an adamantly middle-class novel; a smooth, too plausible Establishment fixer out of C. P. Snow" (229), while a truer, more authentic self enters a scene from the stage of Samuel Beckett, "beyond conversation and invitation, eternally separate" (230). The list of comparisons between the characters of *Daniel Martin* and other artists goes on: Byron, Austen, Kafka, Tolstoy, Rousseau, Manet, Renoir, Vermeer—all make their appearance as analogues for experiences of various characters in the novel. This is not to reiterate the truism that all art is made out of previous art but to claim that the self—here as an explicitly fictional invention—experiences itself within a field of artistically crafted images and scenes.

The creation of the self through artistic making is also a retroactive process—akin to Freud's *Nachträglichkeit* (deferred action), wherein childhood memory traces are reactivated and reinterpreted at a later age[5]—for it is not until he is an adult that Martin can identify a scene from his boyhood in Devon as being like a Brueghel; it is not until he

---

5.   As Freud wrote on 6 December 1896 to Wilhelm Fliess: "I am working on the assumption that our psychical mechanism has come into being by a process of stratification: the material present in the form of memory-traces being subjected from time to time to a *re-arrangement* in accordance with the fresh circumstances to a *re-transcription*" (In LaPlanche and Pontalis). In Strachey and Mosbacher's translation of the letter, the italics do not appear, nor does the prefix "re-" appear in front of "transcription." Freud believed, at this stage, that perception rather than fantasy provided the basis for memory; in this sense, the deferred memory activation would be a *re*-transcription. In any case, the metaphor of transcribing and translation is already well established here: "I must emphasize the fact," Freud writes in the same letter, "that the successive transcripts represent the psychical achievement of successive epochs of life." And: "A failure of translation is what we know clinically as 'repression.' "

develops a sophisticated field of artistic references that this method of resemblances can function effectively to provide him with a new orientation in his life.

The field of art images constitutes a language that consists of a related system of likenesses and differences of various artworks. Saussure, whose work has been so fruitfully expanded by structuralism and poststructuralism, writes that "language is a system of interdependent terms in which the value of each term results solely from the simultaneous presence of the others" (114). Values, in turn, are composed of "a *dissimilar* thing that can be *exchanged* for the thing of which the value is to be determined and . . . of *similar* things that can be *compared* with the thing of which the value is to be determined" (114). Difference is not the only characteristic of a semiotic system; likeness and resemblance, which are vital to the textual layering of *Daniel Martin,* are also an integral aspect of any system of language.

In the case of Martin's perceptions of himself, the elemental signifiers are not phonemes, letters, or words, but various poems, fables, paintings, novels, music, and sculptures. These form, as it were, a second-order semiological system (Barthes's definition of myth). Each work gains its meaning from its position in regard to the other terms, and *Daniel Martin,* for the reader, comes to take its place in the series of artistic terms as well.

Daniel's own existence is illuminated by the artworks that he has encountered, since in them he can see an analogy to his own situation, and analogies are constructions dependent upon both likenesses and dissimilarities. Writing, for him, becomes the process of adding to the language of artistic signifiers, but verbal language on its own cannot represent adequately, much less absolutely, the history of his true self, its loss and recovery. He must resort to fiction and regard the novel as a kind of proleptic anamnesis in which the past is brought forward toward the future in the medium of a present textual telling. "The word," Martin says, "is the most imprecise of signs . . . and it is precisely because I can't really evoke it [his past] in words, can only hope to awaken some analogous experience in other memories and sensitivities, that it must be written" (87).

Words, for the novelist, are used not to capture and define the real (however it might be understood) but to evoke scenes in the reader's imagination; they create a semiotic, fictional simulacrum so that others can enter into an experience that is not literally the author's—there is not the illusion of absolute mimesis and identification—but is somehow *like* the author's.

Arthur Danto has argued that art is "a sort of mirror, not merely in the sense of reflecting an external reality, but as giving me to myself for each self that peers into it, showing me something I could not know without benefit of mirrors" (535). I "become," for the time of my reading, Oedipus, Hamlet, Quixote, Bloom, or Daniel Martin. Such a metamorphosis is not of course a literal becoming, for to take such identifications literally is to cross the boundary into psychosis, in which there is a collapse of the figural meaning into the literal one. What does transpose is a temporary and qualified identification that is "a kind of metaphor, in which the thing said metaphorically to be something else retains its identity under that description" (Danto, 534).

I am, and I am not, Hamlet (and Claudius, the queen, and poor Yorick); and such double vision is essential to symbolic consciousness, to any sort of poetic gnosis. If I begin to act out the role of Hamlet, with its resonances of his limping Theban ancestor, I am then in the grip of a neurosis or worse. The issue is *how* we identify with literary characters. How, to use Lacanian terminology, should we position ourselves in relation to the symbolic dimension, which as infants brought us into the human community via the disrupting power of the signifier? As infants, we are written into culture by the culture; we are inscribed by the symbolic. To what extent is it possible to become writers of our own script?

This is precisely Daniel Martin's question; to recover the lost self is to rewrite the old self into a new, revised text. He is aware that he has long been an effect of unconscious patterns. In a delightfully Lacanian childhood memory, he recalls a woodlark's song "in the distance somewhere, bell-fluting trisyllable, core of green, core of spring-summer, already one of those sounds that creep into the unconscious and haunt one all one's life" (88). (The unconscious is structured around phonemes and trisyllabic noises. Bird song combines with the mother's voice.) In another instance, he remarks that his experience with Nell was formed on a "predisposed Freudian pattern" in which "invention and concealment are as important as reality and honesty" (67).

Writing fiction is the activity par excellence in which there is an interaction between invention, concealment, and self-revelation, and, for Martin, all of the psychoanalytic predispositions become most visible and real through the metaphors of art. Early in the novel, as he is leaving Los Angeles, Dan sees himself as "a fiction, a paper person in someone else's script" (62). When he is in Egypt with Jane, he realizes that "he was approaching a fork, the kind of situation some modern novelists [such as John Fowles] met by writing both roads. For days now he had been split, internally if not outwardly, between a known past and an unknown future. That was where his disturbing feeling of not being his own master, of being a character in someone else's play, came from. The past wrote him; and hatred of change, of burning boats" (542).[6]

If Martin's sense of confinement, of being passively determined by other forces, is expressed by artistic metaphors, so too are his deepest feelings of identity and destiny. Three pivotal examples of art's revelatory and reflective capacities for Martin are Restif de la Bretonne's "romanced autobiography" *Monsieur Nicolas,* Professor Kirnberger's experience of an Egyptian papyrus, and the final scene of the novel in which Martin contemplates a Rembrandt self-portrait. In each case, an artwork acts as an analogy for Dan's identity, not merely as a single individual but as an artist himself and as a political—in the broadest sense of a member of communities—entity. Art, in other words, acts to move Martin beyond a narcissistic point of reference and to mediate between Daniel's private world and the more encompassing realities of temporality and intersubjectivity.

Monsieur Nicolas acts for Martin as an emblem of *la bonne vaux,* "the valley of abundance, the sacred combe" (273), which in turn represents the inward retreat of the writer, "a place outside of the normal world, intensely private and enclosed, intensely green and fertile, numinous, haunted and haunting, dominated by a sense of magic that is also a sense of a mysterious yet profound parity in all existence" (273). Martin then confesses that although such images are found throughout literature, the encounter with Restif was nonetheless "one of those experiences that go well beyond the literary and objective into something like the finding of a lost parent, a lost elder brother" (273).

A good orthodox Freudian, with his master's essay "The Uncanny" in hand, would nod sagely at Martin's simile about the "lost parent," for it is the mother's genitals that are "a valley of abundance" "outside" the normal world—divided from it by the incest taboo—"private and enclosed," "fertile," and "haunting." It is the lost object of the mother—the

---

6. Fowles is working in the same arena, on the enigmatic relationship between life and art, in *The Collector* and *The Magus.* From the latter, when Nicholas and Alison are meeting at last in Regent's Park: "And suddenly the truth came to me, as we stood there, trembling, searching, at our point of fulcrum. There were no watching eyes. The windows were as blank as they looked. The theatre was empty. It was not a theatre" (581). The couple has lived through the theatrics of Bourani, and now have a chance to live a "real" life with one another, away from the gaze of their previous masters. Or not, as they may choose. We cannot know their choice, or their future; they are frozen in the present tense of textuality. Fowles, however, continues to write fiction that reflects on the relationship of art to life.

mother in her ghostly bed, or dead in the reeds near Oxford—that
Martin seeks. Since she, however, is permanently unavailable, he defensively and compensatorily writes his loss in the lines of his self-creating
text. Since it is impossible that he is born from a dead woman, he must
give birth to himself through verbal palingenesis.[7]

The Freudian is of course correct, but for readers and writers every
text is overdetermined and cannot be reduced to the *Vorhof,* the vesti-
bule, of the mother's genitals. Art not only leads backward to childhood
but also confers meaning in the present and draws us into the future
toward our own life and death. Not only is art a defense against the
recognition of loss, but it is also at least a partial resolution of that loss
and a remaking of one's life through its establishment as part of the
artistic order. Intercourse and interdiction are provoked and complemented by intertextuality.

Professor Kirnberger's experience as an Egyptologist shows most succinctly this transfer from the natural to the artistic order. He relates to
Dan and Jane "a last story: a personal one, what he called a ghost story
without a ghost" (524). Previous to this conversation, he had already
declared that time is the source of all human illusion, and that it is
possible, in small part, to overcome time by use of the imagination.

Kirnberger had been working on a wall painting in one of the tombs in
the cliffs across from Aswan when he felt a "curious sense of a living
presence that was not his own" (524). Reflecting further, trying to articulate to the English couple what cannot be adequately said, he continues:
"For a little interval time does not seem to exist. One is neither the
original painter nor one's own self, a modern archaeologist. If one is
anything—I speak metaphorically, forgive me, I lack words to express it
in any other way, one is the painting. One exists, but it is somehow not in
time. In a greater reality, behind the illusion we call time" (525). This is
not a mystical flight that submerges the self into the One, but an

---

7.   This approach places *Daniel Martin* close to the genre of creation myths. It would be
interesting to read this, or similar novels, through the perspective of Lévi-Strauss's presentation
of the Oedipus myth in "The Structural Study of Myth." It is not, however, only a problem of
"how *one* can be born from *two*" (*Structural Anthropology,* 213) but how one can be born
from an absent being nowhere to be found, that is, from the dead. As Ragland-Sullivan writes in
her discussion of Lacan: "The work of mourning is to 'kill the dead,' that is, to detach oneself
from the introjected power of an 'object' who is lost or dead. The (m)Other within is associated with loss and in this sense is half-dead" (JL, 296). The text, as Kristeva suggested (MI), has
become an enactment of mourning. As such, this is an Oedipal mythology experienced from
the child's, perhaps only the male child's, perspective. Things look differently from a mythology
of the mother's.

identification—however it might be rationally explicated—with the timelessness of an artwork.

Martin had already intimated this type of experience with *la bonne vaux* at Thorncombe and Tsankawi, the Pueblo ruins in New Mexico, as well as with the plethora of art images that he uses as analogies to his own life. It is like the relationship of the artist to the artwork in Yeats's "Sailing to Byzantium":

> Once out of nature I shall never take
> My bodily form from any natural thing,
> But such a form as Grecian goldsmiths make
> Of hammered gold and gold enamelling
> To keep a drowsy Emperor awake;
> Or set upon a golden bough to sing
> To lords and ladies of Byzantium
> Of what is past, or passing, or to come.
>
> (lines 25–32)

The artist becomes the work of art that he has produced; Daniel Martin becomes *Daniel Martin*. From that vantage point, apparently timeless, the golden bird (or the novel) can sing of the things of time, of existence within the flux of becoming and dying. But this vision is shot through with illusion, for the fixed moment of vision is just that, a moment, a mere flicker of the eye of the mind.

Time's wheel does not stop. The vision is only for a "little interval" (525); it is both "an infinity and an evanesence" (110). As Martin remarks when he is speaking of the Robin Hood myth, with its green retreats, "the quintessence of *la bonne vaux* is its transience" (275). To struggle to remain in the moment of eternity is to become lost in the wilderness, to stay within the psychotic discourse of the primary processes. It is to stare at oneself in the pool, mesmerized, and therefore to lose any sense of reality except for the mirage in front of one's gaze.

The artist, as artist, does not remain identified with the timeless experience, for that would be ruin for the creation of art. Art, even art that represents the contemplative moment of eternity, exists as a medium of temporality. Time is the author of illusion, and therefore without time there would be no literary work, no fiction of authorship. Without death there would not be the lack, that gap in being, that provokes poiesis.

Kirnberger, like Martin—who has already insisted that time is "the mother of metaphors" (339)—knows this. The Egyptologist struggles with the irresolvable tension between an experience that has radically shaped his perception of life and the words that he must use to speak of the experience. "I speak metaphorically, forgive me," he says, standing at one of the limits, the boundary zones, of mimetic art.

For the writer, whose only work materials are those most imprecise of signs, the silence of the mystic is not an option; paradoxically, even silence must be entered into the ebb and flow of language. Metaphorical speech, of which all fictional discourse partakes, is a talkative representative of silence, of a knowledge that stands between the absolute futility of language and the absolute trust in the fullness of language. It simultaneously says and refrains from saying.

With Kirnberger's recollection of his experience in the tomb, we have approached a kind of vanishing point, an extremity, in terms of the relationship between human existence and that of the art object. The human being passes over from life of growth, decay, and change and becomes reified as a golden bird, a tomb painting, a text. The participle becomes a noun; the verb dies into stasis. Martin himself asks whether the novel is not merely the successor to the pyramids. As K. A. Chittick has noted about this portion of the story, "The narcissistic art of the novel, the attempt to apprehend the *noumena* of existence through a narrative of the *phenomena* of one's life, has become the heir, worthy or not, of the art which narrated a pharaoh's afterlife" (77).

This is not, finally, Fowles-Martin's end point (nor is it mine in this version of revisioning subjectivity in the light of textuality). Somewhere in our thought about art, there must be retained an inherent principle of motion, or all art becomes only a collection of museum pieces: wonderful to contemplate and study, but without its own interior life. The "transience" that allows for knowledge across time and necessitates the creation of metaphor must be remembered and incorporated into the text.

Martin remembers this within the text that bears his name. *Daniel Martin* does not end in Egypt—the land of the dead sacralized by mummification—but in north London with Martin, who, having parted with Jenny, wanders into the Kenwood House where he finds, as if by coincidence, a late Rembrandt self-portrait. Rembrandt, like Martin, is one who knows himself only by creating himself as a work of art. But Rembrandt has himself now become a museum piece, an empty canvas on the wall, until Martin comes to resurrect the Dutchman's self-representation into his own web of significance and meaning.

Rembrandt means a number of things to Martin, as he stands at the cusp between his past and his future. The painting "seemed to denounce" (628) Dan's century, art, and personal being, and it also said all that he was unable to say in words. It stood as a "formidable sentinel guarding the way back" (629), the way "back" to authenticity that is the way forward toward a renewed life. The self-portrait also mingles in Dan's mind with his father's insistence that Christ's eyes followed everywhere, seeing everything.

But Dan's father is dead, and Christ has been transfigured into Rembrandt, whose eyes show the "one true marriage in the mind mankind is allowed. . . . No true compassion without will, no true will without compassion" (629). The authoritative gaze of *the* other—as father, Christ, or superego—is broken, so that the gaze of *an* other—as Rembrandt or Jane—may come more fully into being. Narcissus, by writing an invented tale that makes himself real, has begun to tear his gaze away from the image in the water, to look around—like Oedipus at Colonus—and see what the world has to offer him.

The novel ends with Daniel telling Jane, in her Oxford kitchen, that he had "found a last sentence for the novel he was never going to write. She laughed at such flagrant Irishry; which is perhaps why, in the end, and in the knowledge that Dan's novel can never be read, lies eternally in the future, his ill-concealed ghost has made that impossible last his own impossible first" (629).

That first sentence, "Whole sight; or all the rest is desolation" (3), is impossible for the reason that none of us can know the fullness of insight to which the sentence points. The fantasy of "whole sight" lies too close to Narcissus's fantasy of omnipotence. And yet, *Daniel Martin* does attempt a version of whole sight, for Daniel and Jane open themselves to the knowledge of each other, and the private world of the interior self makes a truce, however uneasy, with the public world of politics and history.

The primary sign of this attempt is that Daniel (through the "ghostly" mediation of John Fowles) transposes himself into a text, a polyphonic and polysemous reality in which many voices are able to be heard through the organization of a central "ego," the writer reflecting upon himself. Both the ego and the many voices of the other are, then, quite real. Reality, however, is not an empirical given that may be unearthed and accurately described in mimetic language, but, as Martin muses as he contemplates returning to England, it is "that ultimate ambiguous fiction of the enacted past" (50). However, from the beginning to the end of the novel, a significant change has occurred in the quality of the fiction that Martin lives.

The determinants of Daniel's fictional self-presentation have been transformed from the repressive power of the compulsion to repeat his past to the liberating power of releasing the past in favor of the present. I concur with Ina Ferris when she claims that "it is through myth rather than history that *Daniel Martin* comes close to transcending its auto-centricity, to reaching beyond the individual consciousness and solipsistic world of its hero" (148).[8] Perhaps, after all, "what Dan always wanted of his looking-glasses was not his own face, but the way through them" (208).

In rewriting the text of himself, in transforming Daniel Martin into *Daniel Martin,* Mr. Specula Speculans has found a way through at least some of his narcissistic mirrors, thereby prying himself away from a relentless and self-destructive infatuation with himself. He has begun to learn that the mirror has more than one facet and that the self cannot be captured in a stare that is forever transfixed upon itself.

8. Ferris concludes her article with the following statement: "In Roman Jakobson's celebrated distinction, Fowles tends to metaphor rather than to metonymy, his imagination working through similitude and analogy rather than through the contiguities and disjunctions of metonymy. But he insists on allying his narrative with the metonymic mode of realism and in so doing resists his own strength" (152). Although I agree with her assessment of Fowles's primary way of imagining, I think that the "alliance" with realistic modes of fiction increases the power and quality of his writing. Myth is clearly the force that drives his writing, but it cannot operate alone. To my mind, *Mantissa,* which comes close to myth (and its parody), is a good example of the failure of Fowles's writing when he abandons the marriage between the two modes (a marriage that is the modus operandi of *Daniel Martin*).

Narcissus in the Theater
of the Other

Does not the metaphoric origin of language lead us necessarily to a situation of threat, distress, and dereliction, to an
archaic solitude, to the anguish of dispersion? Absolute fear
would then be the first encounter of the other as *other,* as
other than I and as other than itself.

—Jacques Derrida

Heil dem Geist, der uns verbinden mag;
denn wir leben wahrhaft in Figuren.

—Rainer Maria Rilke

I n these extended reflections on
Narcissus and textual subjectivity, we have seen how Freud and Lacan
understand the narcissistic position with its wounds, its scars, its ghosts,
its statues and automatons. We have discerned the many guises of Narcissus in *The Waves, The Ogre,* and *Daniel Martin.* In Woolf's novel, Bernard attempted to use writing to capture the fleeting moments of life and
to create a stable identity for himself. As he wrote, however, he came to
realize that the composed self is a self in flux, a self opening up into
nothingness and therefore never completely stabilized. Language and
the world can never cohere into a single epiphanic moment that tri-
umphs over death.

In *The Ogre,* Abel Tiffauges never learns to bridge the gap of metaphor
and thereby learn the difference between artistic and psychotic existence. He lives within the narcissistic grandiosity of the identifications of
the imaginary register of experience, and his sinister writings are a rec-

ord of an internal apocalypse that mirrors precisely the catastrophe of
the Third Reich. Tiffauges is Narcissus always drowning in the cold
waters that lead to the land of the dead.

In the last of the three novels, Daniel Martin learns to rewrite the
script of himself by changing from one art form, that of the screenplay, to
the form of the novel. Through this decision, which leads him back and
down to the phantoms of his past, he writes *Daniel Martin,* the book of
himself. Only as he becomes a kind of work of art himself, does Daniel
Martin begin to come out of the hall of mirrors in which he has been
entrapped and enter the larger texts of North London and Rembrandt's
vision of whole sight.

In this final chapter, then, all that is left is to articulate more fully what
is needed for Narcissus—as a figure for the textualized self and for a
phallo-logocentric culture—to become transformed. But as I write
about transformation, I am well aware that Narcissus is so profoundly
embedded in the cultural texts in which we live that the pattern called
narcissism remains an enduring possibility, and perhaps even a necessity,
of existence. As Freud contends in "One of the Difficulties of Psycho-
Analysis," there is never a time when "the whole of the libido is ever
transferred from the ego to objects outside itself" (350). Psychic and
social life require a degree of self-representation and self-reflexivity; the
question is whether other activities such as love or another form of
vision are possible as well.

In the same essay, Freud connects the pathology of narcissism to a
more general condition of humankind, thereby relocating his work from
the clinical couch to the arena of culture itself. About the first type of
narcissism, he writes that, "the condition in which the libido is contained within the ego is called by us 'narcissism,' in reference to the
Greek myth of the youth Narcissus who remained faithful to his love for
his own reflection. Thus we look upon the development of the individual as a progress from narcissism to object-love" (349–50). This succinctly summarizes the starting point for my analysis of Narcissus and his
difficulties with the task of symbolization.

About the second form of narcissism, Freud observes that the "general
narcissism of man, the self-love of humanity, has up to the present been
three times severely wounded by the researches of science" (350). The
first attack against the "narcissistic illusion" occurred with Copernicus,
the second with Darwin, and the third with the advent of Freud's psychoanalytic method, which demonstrated that "*the ego is not master in its
own house*" (355). The place of human beings in the cosmos, in the
natural order of biology, and then even within the presumably sacro-

sanct arena of the mind itself has been successively disrupted and under-
mined, and Freud considered the most recent blow "probably the most
wounding" (352).

Science, as the representative of the reality principle, has three times
shown humankind the folly of its narcissism. Since Nietzsche and Marx,
philosophy has also contributed to the labor of decentering humanity
from its most cherished illusion, and literature accomplishes a similar
work, especially when it moves from a focus on character and plot to a
focus on the structures of its own medium of existence, language. The
cultural and individual house that the Cartesian ego has built is, like
morning mist over a pool in the forest, evaporating.

And yet there is also a paradox operating in these forms of the
antihumanistic hermeneutics of suspicion, for even though it is in unexpected ways, even they reconstellate narcissism. The "text," which replaces the moribund "author" as the generating site of meanings, tends
to become narcissistically inflated; and Blanchot, for example, advises
that we beware of the "dangerous leaning towards the sanctification of
language" (110). If everything is text, if as Derrida has famously written
"there is nothing outside of the text" (G, 158), then everything becomes
part of the same field of interpretation.

James Hillman has observed that a number of the critics of culture
"have each seen that psychoanalysis breeds a narcissistic subjectivism
inflicting on the culture an iatrogenic disorder, that is, a disease brought
by the methods of the doctors who would cure it" ("Mirror," 63). Psychoanalysis itself, that is, perpetuates the narcissism it attempts to eradicate;
and, analogously, the experimental literature of postmodernism tends to
become as predictable as the most blasé novel of realism.

As I argued in my introduction, when we step into the domain of
Narcissus we step into a particular vision of the world: a reflective vision
of self-images, melancholy, and death, a world that violently excludes the
other in its attempt at self-possession. Narcissism as a structure of consciousness, unconsciousness, and culture is not easily deconstructed or
transcended. Since it has no reference point but itself, it cannot be
overcome from within; since there is no "outside" of narcissism from
within the narcissistic perspective, it cannot be destroyed from without.
The only possibility is that from the gap that metaphorical awareness
learns to cross, from the borderlines and edges of language, Narcissus
might live through to another place of seeing, or to another kind of
seeing that escapes the logic of the all-consuming and death-driven
same. Narcissus is captivated by the image of identity; what other can
appear to lure him away from his autoerotism?

Here we must be wary, for to invoke the logic of the same and the other at this juncture holds dangers as well. If the other becomes valorized in opposition to the same, the other will eventually come to play the same role as its apparent opponent and will become yet another version, a mirror image, of the same. This is the knot that deconstruction is trying to undo as it works within philosophy to overcome philosophy. It is also this love-stricken face of Narcissus that I am here reimagining through Freud, Lacan, Woolf, Tournier, and Fowles.

In "White Mythology," Derrida argues that metaphor always carries death within itself, either "via the Hegelian transcendence of metaphor that ends in the self-consciousness of the Absolute Subject, and thus the destruction of any need for metaphor, or via the Nietzschean route which explodes the reassuring opposition of the metaphoric and the proper, the opposition in which the one and the other have never done anything but reflect and refer to each other in their radiance" (270–71). In addition, a third way leads from one metaphor to another instead of destroying metaphor. Perhaps, this is what Derrida means when he speaks of the "supplement of a code which traverses its own field, endlessly displaces its closure, breaks its line, opens its circle, and no ontology will have been able to reduce it" (271). This path that leads from metaphor to metaphor, without the hope of a conclusion but also without giving up all the distinctions between instances of metaphor, passes in contemporary theory through the defile of structural linguistics and thereby erases the human self as a stable and fixed I and rewrites it as a textual I that is always in process. The word is in motion, and a terrifying exhiliration ensues.

The disciplines that are laboring to put the word back into motion and unreify the subject are the heirs of Nietzsche, Saussure, or Freud. And all of them are working to undo the opposition between the *res cogitans* and the *res extensa* that Descartes established in order to gain "firm and constant knowledge in the sciences" (17) and that was dependent on a bound and self-conscious I in which "thinking" could occur.

Descartes's dualistic philosophy engendered the narcissistic subjectivism that constellates Narcissus as an unavoidable mythologem for modernity in all of its guises. If Narcissus is transformed, Cartesianism, with its legion of implications, will be as well, and it is Lacan who, in his rereading of Freud, most forcibly and clearly disputes Descartes's project of founding knowledge on the indubitability of the I. He emphasizes the mirror stage of psychic development "for the light it sheds on the formation of the 'I' as we experience it in psychoanalysis. It is an experience that leads us to oppose any philosophy directly issuing from the

Cogito" (E, 1).[1] Calling the philosophical *cogito* a "mirage"—a term proper to the reflective reflexivity with which I am concerned—Lacan asks whether the "place that I occupy as the subject of a signifier is concentric or excentric, in relation to the place I occupy as subject of the signified? . . . It is not a question of knowing whether I speak of myself in a way that conforms to what I am, but rather of knowing whether I am the same as that of which I speak" (E, 165). Lacan, of course, demonstrates that the speaking self and the self of which "I" speak are not congruent; an alienating gap separates the *je* and the *moi,* the unified ego and the largely unconscious subject.

He continues: "What one ought to say is: I am not wherever I am the plaything of my thought; I think of what I am where I do not think to think" (E, 166). This position completely reverses the Cartesian *cogito* in which thought and self-identity were conflated; by its introduction of the unconscious, such a reversal gives us a direction for the interpretation of the subtitle of Lacan's essay: "Reason since Freud." Reason, insofar as the term remains meaningful, must now take into account the excentric eccentricity of the unconscious. The mirror of reason, or Descartes's "light of nature," yields both to the sliding signifier and to the lack at the center of human being that forestalls the fulfillment of desire.[2]

This desire is, most fundamentally, the desire for recognition by the other, and it is concerning the category of the other that Lacan makes further remarks about the relationship between Descartes and Freud. Once Descartes has proven to his own satisfaction that he exists as a *res cogitans,* the true still "remains so much outside that Descartes then has to re-assure himself—of what, if not of an Other that is not deceptive" (FFC, 36). For Descartes, reason in the form of the ontological argument leads to the existence of a perfect God, and the existence of a perfect God acts to ground the rational process that itself grounds the certain knowledge of science. The other in its divine perfection stabilizes the entire metaphysical project of self-identity and knowledge of the world.

With the development of psychoanalysis, the situation is radically

---

1. The conjunction of "light" and "subjectivity," as I mentioned in the chapter on Woolf, requires much more extensive work. Lacan himself takes up the subject in *The Four Fundamental Concepts of Psychoanalysis* (67–105), as well as in other of his seminars.

2. This "lack" itself is not a Lacanian invention. Already in the *Symposium,* Plato had said of Eros that it is constituted by lack. But the fact that Lacan is working in a psychoanalytic context rather than the context of idealism makes, literally, a world of difference. As Lacan notes, "And that is why only psychoanalysis allows us to differentiate within memory the function of recollection. Rooted in the signifier, it resolves the Platonic aporias of reminiscence through the ascendancy of history in man" (E, 167).

altered. "I would now like to stress," Lacan remarks, "that the correlative of the subject is henceforth no longer the deceiving Other, but the deceived Other" (FFC, 37). No longer is the problem that there might be, as with Descartes's methodological paranoia, an evil and deceiving spirit, but that the subject itself is always deceived about itself. Self-deception is constitutive of the subject. Subjectivity, because it is founded on the specular image of the other as mirror, is inevitably and always misconstrued and misconceived (*méconnaissance*). The self exists not as the simple self-identity of substance and not as a purely autonomous ego, but rather as a text, as a work of fiction always in progress.

On the one hand, this perspective is pure metaphor, a vision of the human being *as* or *like* a text. The "proper" meaning—since the figurative and the literal are created as an opposition—lies elsewhere, in another model such as a physiological machine; such as that which produces, and is produced by, the structures of the economy; or such as that which creates itself out of a cry of courageous despair. On the other hand, when language is taken as the sine qua non for developing other models of human being, then the textualized subject who writes existence slides in an odd reversal toward the proper site of the literal.

> The human subject is a metaphor, made up of refractive representations, representations which catalyse emotive (Imaginary) responses such as pleasure, boredom, and so on. Text, psyche, and world would be magnetically linked by (repressed, sublimated) representations which, although Real, can only be indirectly expressed by language, while they reverberate enigmatically in the Imaginary perceptual domain. (Ragland-Sullivan, "Prolegomena," 401)

Or, as Lacan himself insisted, "Thus it is from somewhere other than the Reality that it concerns that Truth derives its guarantee: it is from Speech. Just as it is from Speech that Truth receives the mark that establishes it in a fictional structure" (E, 306).

Because we are oriented by and within language, fictionality becomes the essence of the human, and literature acts as the exemplary token of this essence. But since this fictionality is catalyzed by the mirror of the other, by the arbitrary relationship between signifier and signified, and by the abyss that separates the two and forces all awareness to pass through the "defile of the signifier," it is not an "essence" in the classical sense. Although the essence always occurs and is the ambience in which human life is constituted, its paradoxical effect is to de-essentialize itself and set the subject adrift in freedom. And freedom, in turn, is the medium in which existential poiesis, the making of a life as narrative, occurs.

But the free making of a life as a piece of fiction—a patchwork of aphorisms rather than an imposing set of gilt-edged and leather-bound collected works—occurs within constraints. We are constrained by the very thing that also empowers us: the other in its many guises. Not only do we not know language as an object we can intellectually encompass (as *langue* or *logos*), we do not even have mastery of our "own" speech. Our tongues slip, we repeat ourselves without knowing it, we rattle on in meaningless and idle chatter. Freud calls this mark of constraint "castration"; Lacan, the "cut." Another name for it is finitude, in which lurks the quiet whisper of death.

It is otherness as language, person, the unconscious, and death that Narcissus refuses to open himself to as he stares at himself, reflected and unattainable, in the pool. He longs to be both subject and object of his own desire, and not to be riddled by the necessity of symbolization and the desire of an other. He wants wanting to be contained within the dyadic space of his own self-consciousness and strenuously resists being broken open by a third perspective, which is the necessary movement of any awareness of the symbolic. The two must become three if significance and meaning are to be generated. The mother-child dyad is shattered by the Law of the Father; the signifier and signified must be taken up by interpretation.

Narcissus wants love to flow within an identity that is doubled and comes to mimic a lovely couple enraptured by each other's beauty that remains always just beyond the reach of the extended, trembling fingers. He wants the erotic connection to be one of identification, which occurs in the Lacanian imaginary, rather than one of symbolic action, whose work always involves a third: death.

As Lacan contends in his reading of the game of *fort-da*, the death of the thing, the object of perception and love, gives rise to the signifying life of symbols. One mask of death is language itself, with its capacity to tell stories and to offer the conditions for the possibility of works such as *The Waves, The Ogre,* and *Daniel Martin.* All of these are, in a certain sense, ghost stories told by and about the phantoms that haunt narcissistic experience. Fiction raises the dead to life by the action of third parties called writers and readers. Even in the most "realistic" fiction, therefore, the mimetic act of writing can never be a simple reflective representation by language of the things of the world. Such a fantasy of representation forgets the necessary third term; it forgets, like Narcissus himself, that the mirror is always mirrored.[3]

Death also appears as a psychoanalyst. Lacan writes in "The Freudian Thing" that "the analyst intervenes concretely in the dialectic of analysis by pretending he is dead, by cadaverizing his position as the Chinese say, either by his silence when he is the Other with a capital O, or by annulling his own resistance when he is the other with a small o. In either case, and under the respective effects of the symbolic and the imaginary, he makes death present" (E, 140). The psychoanalyst is dead because he or she does not respond as the analysand expects. Perhaps the only response is unnerving silence, but in any case the narcissistic expectations of the analysand will not be directly met. The analyst does not hear what the analysand thinks is spoken, but something else in which the position of the third term is "filled" by the voice of the unconscious.

Kristeva fills out the place of the third term with the father, who "introduces the Third Party as a condition of psychic life, to the extent that it is a loving life." The mother will "love her child with respect to that Other, and it is through a discourse aimed at that Third Party that the child will be set up as 'loved' for the mother" (TL, 34).[4] Here, as in the other examples of the representatives of death and the transposition of death into writing, the third party both constrains the narcissism of the child and gives the child a way to move beyond narcissism by the entrance of the subject into the symbolic world of discourse and culture.

The unconscious also acts to "fill" the third position in the dialectic of symbolism. As Lacan notes, "It is therefore in the position of a third term that the Freudian discovery of the unconscious becomes clear as to its true grounding" (E, 49). The unconscious, structured like a language, is not available to the subject attempting to construct his or her history through the work of psychoanalysis; it is an immanently transcendent

---

3. Eros again. Plato's metaphysics often bears the brunt of our fantasies of "bad" systems of representation. There are some good reasons for this—for example, as regards the questions of gender—but in his struggle to understand the relationship between the Forms and sensible objects, Plato did have a sense of a third term. Socrates asks Diotima what power Eros possesses, and she replies, "Interpreting and communicating human affairs to the gods and divine matters to men.... Being in the middle, it fulfills both, and in this way unites the whole with itself" (*Symposium*, 80). Eros is thus a hermeneutical principle.

4. This is a point over which both Lacan and Kristeva have been critiqued by feminism. It seems to me that the important thing is that the third position of the symbolic is "filled" by a real person, not whether that person is male or female (though this will have its own consequences as well).

reality that acts—backstage, so to speak—to reconnect the subject with the object.

With the generation of the speech of the unconscious that moves between the cadaverous analyst and the analysand learning to talk freely, there is an accompanying generation of love as both transference and as the erotic reconnection between the subject and the objects of desire. Slowly the "censored chapter," which is the unconscious that has been "written down elsewhere" (E, 50) than in my conscious awareness, can be rewritten. A page of glory or shame can be added, letter by letter, to form the text that is my self.

Death, the psychoanalyst, the law of culture represented by a parental figure, the unconscious—all act to fill the empty slot of the archetypal structure of the third. But "filling a slot," even with its reminder of the nothingness that is the a priori prerequisite of symbolism and the sexuality that the "filling" involves, is too static a concept to use in this context, for the action of the third *generates* meanings and the possibility of human identity. And meaning is incessantly in motion.

It is the acceptance of the third term necessary to symbolic interaction that holds the possibility of transforming Narcissus. Narcissus refuses the presence of the third party because it entails surrendering the delights of the imaginary—even the hidden and masochistic delights of the painful love unreturned by the beautiful image in the pool—for the constrictions of the symbolic world. Resisting the love of those who long for his touch, resisting the capture of his own desire by that of another, Narcissus is trapped in his own reflective self-reflexivity.

Ovid writes that when Narcissus first fell in love with himself, he saw

> An image in the pool, and fell in love
> With that unbodied hope, and found a substance
> In what was only shadow. He looks in wonder,
> Charmed by himself, spell-bound, and no more moving
> Than any marble statue.   (lines 420–24)

Shadows and statues, the insubstantial and the rigid, are two related forms of narcissism.[5] Narcissus's love is a bodiless love, without hope of sexual consummation. It is also a love without the hope of the symbolic intercourse of speech, for the image cannot respond to Narcissus's verbal entreaties. This dislocation, as John Brenkman has observed, leads to

5. See my discussion in the chapter on Lacan of phantoms, statues, and the automatons.

Narcissus's recognition that he is staring at an image of himself: "The image reproduces the visible, exterior signs of speech—the movement of Narcissus's lips—but not the sound of the voice. The image gives *signa* but not *verba*. It is only when Narcissus articulates this breach between image and voice that he makes the crucial statement about the self: 'iste ego sum.' 'I am that one' " (312). But though in a sense "I am that one" of the image, in another equally true sense, "I am not that one." The one that speaks is not spoken back to; the monologue of Narcissus never becomes dialogue. As I have been arguing, it depends upon where the I and the other are situated. Better yet, "to articulate the breach" is to write oneself as a fictional subject; it is to accept difference and nothingness as the strangely necessary elements of subjectivity. Brenkman continues: "The drama of Narcissus . . . puts the self in primordial relation to its other, to spatiality, to death, to 'writing.' It is not simply a drama of the same reproduced as nonidentical, but the same *produced* as nonidentical to itself" (320).

The narcissist, unwilling to embrace the other that pries the self away from itself, encounters the other as a blow to the heart or to the back of the head, a blow from nowhere that breaks the body and drags the autoerotic subject down to the vaporous domain of the shades. We are all, as both Freud and Lacan demonstrate, narcissists; and we are all, as Derrida suggests in the epigraph to this chapter, terrified of the other because it brings with it the dispersion of our unified self-concepts. The textual ficticity of being a subject, subject to language and its play of metaphor, entails within itself the fear of being erased. Yet that which is erased must first be written.

It all seems so easy. Why can't Narcissus simply turn from the absorption in his fantasy to Echo with her arms outstretched? And even if he cannot turn to her because of his "hard pride," cannot we employ Echo as a representative for the other that, by setting the dialectic of symbolization in motion, frees Narcissus from the mesmerizing gaze of Thanatos disguised as desire?

Only provisionally. Within the Ovidian context, although he experiences several metamorphoses of form, Narcissus is not transformed. Even when he dies and descends to Hades, he finds "a pool to gaze in, / Watching his image in the Stygian water" (lines 502–3). His shade desires the image of a shade. And when his would-be lovers come to bury him, they find "nothing, / Only a flower with a yellow center / Surrounded with white petals" (lines 508–10). The flower itself is not a transformation of Narcissus's nature, but rather "a substitution '*pro corpore*,' '*in place of* the body' " (Brenkman, 326).

Echo's love is not efficacious for Narcissus within Ovid's text. But what about within the twentieth-century text I am constructing using words from psychoanalysis, literature, and philosophy? Cannot "woman" in the shape of Echo provide the third term, the disquieting other who lures "man" from his obsession with the selfsame of patriarchy, who liberates man from his ocular possession of and by himself?[6]

No. In the first place, if woman is imagined as Echo and then valorized as the other, the dialectic of the same and other continues unabated. The poles of the binary opposites might become reversed, but the categories themselves would not change. Second, Echo—herself wounded by her position between Juno and Jove's erotic battles—can only repeat the last words said in a "sort of nondialogue: not the language whence the Other would have approached him, but only the mimetic, rhyming alliteration of a semblance of language" (Blanchot, 127). Echo's words are not yet a language; because of the loss she has suffered at Juno's hands, Narcissus can only hear, in an auditory equivalent of his vision in the pool, himself.

By his very way of being himself, Narcissus cannot admit an other into the structure of his subjectivity. In fact, the "drama of Echo in its entirety—the dialogue of self and other, the other as another autonomous subject, the possibility of reciprocal desire—is inscribed within the drama of Narcissus: as Narcissus's illusion" (Brenkman, 321). Since Narcissus is not yet broken and liberated by a third party, he cannot even recognize the presence of an other, but automatically remolds every perception into an image of himself. If the contemporary Narcissist takes woman, as Echo, to be the hinge that will free him, Echo will only be rewritten into his own self-styled drama, a drama with only one character. Just as in Ovid, she will not only lose the free use of her creative voice, but she will also sacrifice her body to his refusal to initiate or accept desire in the context of otherness.

To be transformed, Narcissus must accept the third term of otherness that is necessary to symbolization. But Narcissus, as Narcissus, is unable to do just this. It is here that the process of writing a new page of the myth must occur, and what is to be written in the contemporary drama of culture—in literature, psychoanalysis, philosophy, and everyday life—cannot be predicted before it is written. But there are, perhaps, some conditions for writing that we can ascertain.

If Narcissus is to learn how to symbolize, and therefore how to become erotically connected with the world and other people, he must

6. For an astute discussion of this question, see Luce Irigaray's *Speculum of the Other Woman*.

learn to become a word, an actor on a different stage than the one to which he is accustomed, and instead of an all-consuming eye, a body. Narcissus wants love to consist of the union of himself with his image, without the presence of the gap that keeps the two halves of the presumed whole in tension. On the basis of this desire, this erotic and imaginary fantasy, he cannot enter into the Echo chamber of a shared language that, as Saussure and others have shown, is based on a system of differences at each level of linguistic performance.

To exclude otherness is to exclude language and to fail to gain entry into the symbolic world of culture. Narcissus creates his own absolute isolation, and as his libido is withdrawn from the world, he withers into himself and passes away. Narcissus wants to be a signifier and a signified that perfectly, without loss or distortion, mirror each other. He wants the bar of which Lacan speaks to dissolve so that the full consummation of his autoerotism may sparkle in the pool of his own eye.

Only when Narcissus becomes a word—when the third term of a referent or an interpretant is added—does transformation occur. And a word cannot stand alone; it is always an "intersubjective" event with its histories, its traces of differences, and its power to combine with other words to form a text. But a "text" from this perspective is not another example of a narcissistic phenomenon; it does not specularly represent a *monolithos,* a single meaning inscribed in stone upon the mountain. It is the text of a play, a theatrical production of truths and illusions, of showing truths through an enacted chiaroscuro of light and shadow. It is an embodied fiction. Narcissus, once he begins to see with the third eye of the symbolic, becomes a text that must be acted and in motion.

Upon what stage is the play presented? No longer does it appear upon the narcissistic stage of the self-identity of consciousness, for "the home of meaning is not consciousness but something other than consciousness" (Ricoeur, 55).[7] The play is no longer the play of the ego, with its self-reflections and self-representations, but a play of the subject founded on the other of culture and the unconscious. "Since Freud," Lacan reminds us, "the unconscious has been a chain of signifiers that somewhere (on another stage, in another scene, he wrote) is repeated, and insists on interfering in the breaks offered it by the effective discourse and the cogitation that it informs" (E, 297).

7.   This remark comes in the context of Ricoeur's discussion of the two modes of hermeneutics, those of suspicion and those that work to restore the fullness of meaning. Ricoeur suggests that the "sacred" may be another name for this "home" of meaning. My thinking on narcissism has been far more influenced by *Freud and Philosophy* than would seem to be the case from my scattered references to it.

The theater that Narcissus constructs on his way toward becoming other than himself is, then, one of interference and of the unexpected. It is no longer the tired melodrama of unrequited love for the beautiful image, but a play that works around the "irremediably ridiculous side to the relations that the unconscious maintains with its linguistic roots" (E, 309). When Narcissus becomes an actor,

> he does this in a language that allows his discourse to be understood by his contemporaries, and which furthermore presupposes their present discourse. Thus it happens that the recitation of the *epos* may include a discourse of earlier days in its own archaic, even foreign language, or may even pursue its course in present time with all the animation of the actor; but it is like an indirect discourse, isolated in quotation marks within the thread of the narration, and, if the discourse is played out, it is on a stage implying the presence not only of the chorus, but also of spectators. (E, 47)

Narcissus can now learn, slowly to be sure, to speak a language that is a true language instead of the private pseudo-language of an introspective and internal dyad, simultaneously grandiose about its pretensions and terrified by the lurking presence of the other. But this education of his elocutionary abilities proceeds through the process of familiarizing himself with the foreign and archaic language of the unconscious. In his new role, the spectacle of self-observation becomes the presence of the chorus—his companions in suffering and the voice of the public—and the spectators, those who will be purged of pity and fear by his performance.

But after the dispersion of pity and fear? A certain kind of drunken laughter erupts that Narcissus has never before known. Speaking about his own political situation in the psychoanalytic "community," Lacan writes, "But if the truth of the subject, even when he is in the position of master, does not reside in himself, but... in an object that is, of its nature, concealed, to bring this object out into the light of day is really and truly the essence of comedy" (FFC, 5). Narcissus's position is analogous, and once he gives up the position of master, he can begin to learn to laugh.[8]

I have argued that for Narcissus to be transfigured, he must learn to

---

8.   Hermann Hesse's *Steppenwolf* is one novel that tells the tale of the narcissistic ego's journey into laughter, a journey accomplished only by entrance into the "Magic Theater" in which the self becomes plural.

play a text within the symbolic, a role that involves becoming a word among words, and he must be willing to shift the stage of the drama from that of the ego to that of the subject. He must at last also become a body, a *corpus,* instead of merely an all-consuming eye that devours its object, which is the reflection of himself. When Narcissus begins to write himself as a different text and to become an actor on the different stage, this "going on stage is like a *rite de passage,* a transition into death" (Hillman, *Dream,* 107).

No longer will Narcissus cry, "If I could only / Escape from my own body!" (Ovid, lines 468–69). Instead, he will take upon himself the mortal coil required of an actor in the drama of subjectivity. This coil is language as body, for as Lacan observes, reminding us that rhetoric is earthy: "Speech is in fact a gift of language, and language is not immaterial. It is a subtle body, but body it is. Words are trapped in all the corporeal images that captivate the subject; they may make the hysteric 'pregnant,' be identified with the object of *penis-neid,* represent the flood of urine of urethral ambition, or the retained faeces of avaricious *jouissance*" (E, 87). Narcissus shifts the cathexis of his libido from his own self-representation to a textual body that enters the chain of signification and thus becomes interpretable. The earthiness of language brings him closer to the body of the world.

Instead of falling through melancholy and the withering away of the body into Hades, when Narcissus consents to become a living body, he immediately brings death close to hand in an entirely different sense. Death lies within the spaces between the words of the textual subject; the nothingness of its dark obscurity inheres in the black letters on the page. Writing always contains within itself the skull.

When Narcissus moves from the imaginary register of reflexive mirroring to the symbolic dimension of subjectivity that acknowledges the necessity of otherness, the body emerges from the chrysalis of reflection, and at the same time, death appears. But death is that very absence upon which signification is constructed; it is what enables reading and writing to be born. "Reflection must become interpretation," Ricoeur contends, "because I cannot grasp the act of existing except in signs scattered in the world" (46). Narcissus sacrifices the ever-insubstantial hope of immediate self-possession for the uncertainties of a career in the theater— with its choruses and chorus lines, its producers and directors, its makeup and lights, its tricks of perception, and its fickle audience. The script has not been written, it is being written. The drama of textual subjectivity is an improvisation.

Narcissus, then, is initially unable to symbolize and is therefore unable to exist as a subject. Caught in the gap between signifier and signified, he cannot see the gap, and therefore cannot take the nothingness of the gap into account and do the work of metaphor. Boaz cannot become the sheaf; fact cannot become meaning; sound cannot become word; vision cannot become embodied.

Through a process of education that involves, in this instance, thinking about psychoanalysis and literature, Narcissus may perhaps realize that "authenticity is the perpetual dismemberment of being and not-being a self, a being that is always in many parts, like a dream with a full cast. . . . Authenticity is *in* the illusion, playing it, seeing through it from within as we play it, like an actor who sees through his mask and can only see in this way" (Hillman, *Healing Fiction,* 39). Appearance does not give way to a fixed reality; from within appearances, like the gods hidden within the Sileni, another appearance appears. No longer is it a vision in which one mirror flatly reproduces a perfect image of an original thing—such as the "self"—that truly exists in an immutable world.

Musing on the ways in which our image of narcissism might itself be changed, Kristeva remarks that

> when behaviors and institutions will have integrated the failure of representation not as a misfire on the part of the machine or a suffering of the individual, but as an illusion among others, a new adjustment of narcissism will have been effected. . . . It will actualize the seeming, the imagination. For such an open, undecidable psychic space, the crisis will not be a suffering but a sign within a framework whose truth lies in its ability to absorb seemings. (TL, 380–81)

Narcissus must struggle through the imaginary to the productive work of the imagination, a work that includes textuality, death and the body, and the illusions of fictionality that sometimes speak the truth.

At this point, the mummy that every narcissist is can change into a mummer; the pale marble statue can take on flesh and blood. Nietzsche, here, as so often, our precursor in thought, is speaking to philosophers, but he could be speaking to everyone who has deadened the zones of desire in order to become a functioning ego in society, when he quips, "Be a philosopher, be a mummy, represent monotono-theism by a gravedigger-mimicry! And away, above all, with the *body,* that pitiable *idée fixe* of the senses! infected with every error of logic there is, refuted, impossible even, notwithstanding it is impudent enough to behave as if it actually existed" (*Twilight,* 35). When the mummy cloth begins to unwind, Narcissus can begin to awake from a long hallucination called "identity" and "autoerotic possession." Desire and the words of desire will begin again to circulate like blood, like moving waters.

Erasing himself as an object of identifications and self-absorption, Narcissus rewrites himself as an actor with a traveling troupe. As a word among words, he stops being himself, stops being Narcissus. Who does he become? What is his new name? To discover that, we will have to enter the darkened, hastily erected theater, rub our hands on the scuffed stage, and—slowly drawing a mask toward our face—begin to lift one foot, then another.

Works Cited

Alter, Robert. "*Daniel Martin* and the Mimetic Task." In *Critical Essays on John Fowles,* ed. Ellen Pifer. Boston: G. K. Hall, 1986.

Baker, James R. "An Interview with John Fowles." *Michigan Quarterly Review* (Fall 1986): 661–83.

Bal, Mieke. "Myth *á la lettre.*" In *Discourse in Psychoanalysis and Literature,* ed. Shlomith Rimmon-Kenan. London: Methuen, 1987.

Barthes, Roland. "The Structuralist Activity." In *The Structuralists: From Marx to Lévi-Strauss,* ed. Richard De George and Fernande M. De George. New York: Anchor Books, 1972.

Benveniste, Emile. *Problems in General Linguistics.* Trans. Mary Elizabeth Meek. Coral Gables, Fla.: University of Miami Press, 1971.

Blanchot, Maurice. *The Writing of the Disaster.* Trans. Ann Smock. Lincoln: University of Nebraska Press, 1986.

Blumenberg, Hans. *Work on Myth.* Trans. Robert Wallace. Cambridge, Mass.: MIT Press, 1985.

Boone, Joseph. "The Meaning of Elvedon in *The Waves:* A Key to Bernard's Experience and Woolf's Vision." *Modern Fiction Studies* 27 (Winter 1981–82): 629–37.

Borges, Jorge. *Labyrinths: Selected Stories and Other Writings.* Ed. Donald Yates and James Irby. New York: New Directions, 1964.

Boyd, Michael. *The Reflexive Novel: Fiction as Critique.* Lewisburg, Pa.: Bucknell University Press, 1983.

Brenkman, John. "Narcissus in the Text." *Georgia Review* 30 (1976): 293–327.

Brooks, Peter. "The Idea of a Psychoanalytic Literary Criticism." In *Discourse in Psychoanalysis and Literature,* ed. Shlomith Rimmon-Kenan. London: Methuen, 1987.

Cahoone, Lawrence E. *The Dilemma of Modernity: Philosophy, Culture, and Anti-Culture.* Albany: State University of New York Press, 1988.

Cassirer, Ernst. *Language and Myth.* Trans. Susanne Langer. New York: Dover Publications, 1946.

Chittick, K. A. "The Laboratory of Narrative and John Fowles's *Daniel Martin.*" *English Studies in Canada* 11 (March 1985): 70–81.

Cook, Albert. *Myth and Language.* Bloomington: Indiana University Press, 1980.

Corngold, Stanley. "Freud as a Literary Text?" *Diacritics* (March 1979): 84–94.

Danto, Arthur. "Some Reflections on Literature and Life." In *Funktionen des Fiktiven,* ed. Dieter Henrich and Wolfgang Iser. Munich: Wilhelm Fink Verlag, 1983.

Delcourt, Xavier. "Michel Tournier 'Dans le mythe se conjugent roman et philosophie.'" *La Quinzaine Littéraire,* 1–15 March 1977, 25.

Derrida, Jacques. *Dissemination.* Trans. Barbara Johnson. Chicago: University of Chicago Press, 1981.

———. *Of Grammatology.* Trans. Gayatri Chakravorty Spivak. Baltimore: Johns Hopkins University Press, 1976.

———. "Structure, Sign, and Play in the Discourse of the Human Sciences." In *Writing and Difference,* trans. Alan Bass. Chicago: University of Chicago Press, 1978.

———. "White Mythology: Metaphor in the Text of Philosophy." In *Margins of Philosophy,* trans. Alan Bass. Chicago: University of Chicago Press, 1972.

Descartes, René. *Meditations on First Philosophy.* Trans. Laurence J. Lafleur. New York: Macmillan, 1960.

Dick, Susan. "I Remembered, I Forgotten: Bernard's Final Soliloquy in *The Waves.*" *Modern Language Studies* 13 (Summer 1983): 38–52.

Dunne, Carrin. "The Roots of Memory." *Spring* 48 (1988): 113–28.

Eco, Umberto. *Semiotics and the Philosophy of Language.* Bloomington: Indiana University Press, 1986.

Felman, Shoshana. "On Reading Poetry: Reflections on the Limits and Possibilities of Psychoanalytical Approaches." In *The Literary Freud: Mechanisms of Defense and the Poetic Will,* ed. Joseph Smith. New Haven, Conn.: Yale University Press, 1980.

———. "The Originality of Jacques Lacan." *Poetics Today* 2(1b) (1980–81): 45–57.

Fenichel, Otto. *The Psychoanalytic Theory of Neurosis.* New York: W. W. Norton, 1945.

Ferris, Ina. "Realist Intention and Mythic Impulse in Daniel Martin." *Journal of Narrative Technique* 12(2) (Spring 1982): 146–53.

Fowles, John. *Daniel Martin.* Boston: Little, Brown, 1977.

———. "Hardy and the Hag." In *Thomas Hardy after Fifty Years,* ed. Lance St. John Butler. London: Macmillan, 1977.

———. *The Magus.* Boston: Little, Brown, 1965.

———. "Notes on an Unfinished Novel." In *Afterwards: Novelists on Their Novels,* ed. Thomas McCormack. New York: Harper & Row.

———. *The Tree.* Boston: Little, Brown, 1980.

Freud, Sigmund. *Beyond the Pleasure Principle.* Trans. James Strachey. New York: W. W. Norton, 1961.

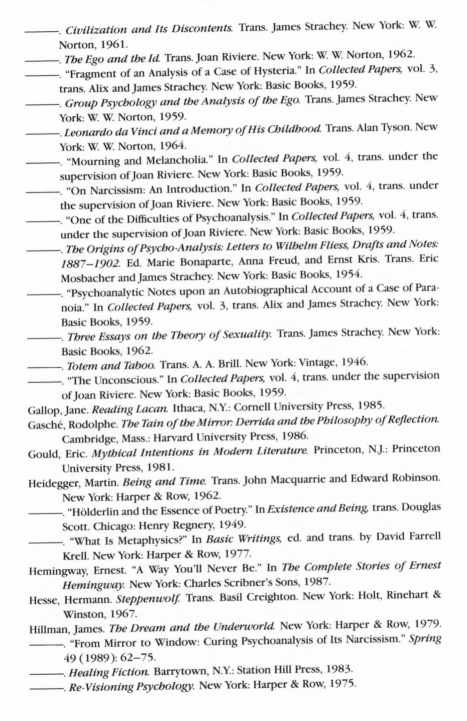

———. *Civilization and Its Discontents.* Trans. James Strachey. New York: W. W. Norton, 1961.

———. *The Ego and the Id.* Trans. Joan Riviere. New York: W. W. Norton, 1962.

———. "Fragment of an Analysis of a Case of Hysteria." In *Collected Papers,* vol. 3, trans. Alix and James Strachey. New York: Basic Books, 1959.

———. *Group Psychology and the Analysis of the Ego.* Trans. James Strachey. New York: W. W. Norton, 1959.

———. *Leonardo da Vinci and a Memory of His Childhood.* Trans. Alan Tyson. New York: W. W. Norton, 1964.

———. "Mourning and Melancholia." In *Collected Papers,* vol. 4, trans. under the supervision of Joan Riviere. New York: Basic Books, 1959.

———. "On Narcissism: An Introduction." In *Collected Papers,* vol. 4, trans. under the supervision of Joan Riviere. New York: Basic Books, 1959.

———. "One of the Difficulties of Psychoanalysis." In *Collected Papers,* vol. 4, trans. under the supervision of Joan Riviere. New York: Basic Books, 1959.

———. *The Origins of Psycho-Analysis: Letters to Wilhelm Fliess, Drafts and Notes: 1887–1902.* Ed. Marie Bonaparte, Anna Freud, and Ernst Kris. Trans. Eric Mosbacher and James Strachey. New York: Basic Books, 1954.

———. "Psychoanalytic Notes upon an Autobiographical Account of a Case of Paranoia." In *Collected Papers,* vol. 3, trans. Alix and James Strachey. New York: Basic Books, 1959.

———. *Three Essays on the Theory of Sexuality.* Trans. James Strachey. New York: Basic Books, 1962.

———. *Totem and Taboo.* Trans. A. A. Brill. New York: Vintage, 1946.

———. "The Unconscious." In *Collected Papers,* vol. 4, trans. under the supervision of Joan Riviere. New York: Basic Books, 1959.

Gallop, Jane. *Reading Lacan.* Ithaca, N.Y.: Cornell University Press, 1985.

Gasché, Rodolphe. *The Tain of the Mirror: Derrida and the Philosophy of Reflection.* Cambridge, Mass.: Harvard University Press, 1986.

Gould, Eric. *Mythical Intentions in Modern Literature.* Princeton, N.J.: Princeton University Press, 1981.

Heidegger, Martin. *Being and Time.* Trans. John Macquarrie and Edward Robinson. New York: Harper & Row, 1962.

———. "Hölderlin and the Essence of Poetry." In *Existence and Being,* trans. Douglas Scott. Chicago: Henry Regnery, 1949.

———. "What Is Metaphysics?" In *Basic Writings,* ed. and trans. by David Farrell Krell. New York: Harper & Row, 1977.

Hemingway, Ernest. "A Way You'll Never Be." In *The Complete Stories of Ernest Hemingway.* New York: Charles Scribner's Sons, 1987.

Hesse, Hermann. *Steppenwolf.* Trans. Basil Creighton. New York: Holt, Rinehart & Winston, 1967.

Hillman, James. *The Dream and the Underworld.* New York: Harper & Row, 1979.

———. "From Mirror to Window: Curing Psychoanalysis of Its Narcissism." *Spring* 49 (1989): 62–75.

———. *Healing Fiction.* Barrytown, N.Y.: Station Hill Press, 1983.

———. *Re-Visioning Psychology.* New York: Harper & Row, 1975.

Hutcheon, Linda. *Narcissistic Narrative: The Metafictional Paradox.* New York: Methuen, 1984.

Irigaray, Luce. *Speculum of the Other Woman.* Trans. Gillian C. Gill. Ithaca, N.Y.: Cornell University Press, 1985.

Jameson, Fredric. *The Prison-House of Language.* Princeton, N.J.: Princeton University Press, 1972.

Jung, C. G. *Memories, Dreams, Reflections.* Ed. Aniela Jaffe. Trans. Richard Winston and Clara Winston. New York: Vintage, 1965.

———. *Psychology and Alchemy.* Trans. R.F.C. Hull. Princeton, N.J.: Princeton University Press, 1968.

———. *Symbols of Transformation.* Trans. R.F.C. Hull. Princeton, N.J.: Princeton University Press, 1956.

Kant, Immanuel. *Critique of Pure Reason.* Trans. Norman Kemp Smith. New York: St. Martin's Press, 1965.

Kellman, Steve. *The Self-Begetting Novel.* New York: Columbia University Press, 1980.

Kristeva, Julia. "On the Melancholic Imaginary." Trans. Louise Burchill. In *Discourse in Psycho-analysis and Literature,* ed. Shlomith Rimmon-Kenan. London: Methuen, 1987.

———. *Tales of Love.* Trans. Leon S. Roudiez. New York: Columbia University Press, 1987.

Lacan, Jacques. *Ecrits: A Selection.* Trans. Alan Sheridan. New York: W. W. Norton, 1977.

———. *The Four Fundamental Concepts of Psycho-Analysis.* Ed. Jacques-Alain Miller. Trans. Alan Sheridan. New York: W. W. Norton, 1978.

———. *The Seminar of Jacques Lacan: Book I, Freud's Papers on Technique 1953–1954.* Ed. Jacques-Alain Miller. Trans. John Forrestor. New York: W. W. Norton, 1988.

LaPlanche, Jean, and J.-B. Pontalis. *The Language of Psycho-analysis.* Trans. Donald Nicholson-Smith. New York: W. W. Norton, 1973.

Lévi-Strauss, Claude. *The Jealous Potter.* Trans. Benedicte Chorier. Chicago: University of Chicago Press, 1988.

———. *The Raw and the Cooked.* Trans. Denver Lindley. Chicago: University of Chicago Press, 1969.

———. *The Savage Mind.* Chicago: University of Chicago Press, 1966.

———. *Structural Anthropology.* Trans. Clari Jacobson and Brooke Grundfest Schoepf. New York: Anchor Books, 1967.

McGrath, William. *Freud's Discovery of Psychoanalysis: The Politics of Hysteria.* Ithaca, N.Y.: Cornell University Press, 1986.

Miller, Alice. *The Drama of the Gifted Child: The Search for the True Self.* Trans. Ruth Ward. New York: Basic Books, 1981.

Miller, David L. "Through a Looking-Glass—The World as Enigma." *Eranos Jahrbuch* 55 (1986): 349–402.

Naremore, James. *The World without a Self: Virginia Woolf and the Novel.* New Haven, Conn.: Yale University Press, 1973.

Nietzsche, Friedrich. *The Birth of Tragedy.* In *Basic Writings of Nietzsche,* ed. and trans. Walter Kaufmann. New York: Modern Library, 1968.

————. "On Truth and Lie in an Extra-Moral Sense." In *Deconstruction in Context: Literature and Philosophy,* ed. Mark Taylor. Chicago: University of Chicago Press, 1986.

————. *Twilight of the Idols.* Trans. R. J. Hollingdale. New York: Viking Penguin, 1987.

Ovid. *Metamorphoses.* Trans. Rolfe Humphries. Bloomington: Indiana University Press, 1964.

Plato. *The Symposium.* Trans. Suzy Q. Groden. Amherst: University of Massachusetts Press, 1970.

Petit, Susan. "Fugal Structure, Nestorianism, and St. Christopher in Michel Tournier's *Le Roi des Aulnes,*" *Novel* 19 (1986): 232–45.

Ragland-Sullivan, Ellie. *Jacques Lacan and the Philosophy of Psychoanalysis.* Urbana: University of Illinois Press, 1987.

————. "The Magnetism between Reader and Text: Prolegomena to a Lacanian Poetics." *Poetics* 13 (1984): 381–406.

Ricoeur, Paul. *Freud and Philosophy.* Trans. Denis Savage. New Haven, Conn.: Yale University Press, 1970.

Saussure, Ferdinand de. *Course in General Linguistics.* Trans. Wade Baskin. New York: McGraw-Hill, 1959.

Schaub, Uta Liebmann. "Foucault's Oriental Subtext." *PMLA* 104(3) (May 1989): 306–16.

Schlack, Beverly Ann. *Continuing Presences: Virginia Woolf's Use of Literary Allusion.* University Park, Pa.: Pennsylvania State University Press, 1979.

Singh, Raman. "An Encounter with John Fowles." *Journal of Modern Literature* 8 (2) (1980–81): 181–202.

Sonoda, Muneto. "Zwischen Denken und Dichten: Zur Weltstruktur des 'Zarathustra.'" *Nietzsche Studien* (1972): 234–47.

Steiner, George. "Narcissus and Echo: A Note on Current Arts of Reading." *American Journal of Semiotics* 1(1–2) (1981): 1–14.

Taylor, Mark. *Altarity.* Chicago: University of Chicago Press, 1987.

Tillich, Paul. *Shaking the Foundations.* New York: Charles Scribner's Sons, 1948.

Tournier, Michel. *The Ogre.* Trans. Barbara Bray. New York: Pantheon Books, 1972.

————. *The Wind Spirit: An Autobiography.* Trans. Arthur Goldhammer. Boston: Beacon Press, 1988.

Vinge, Louise. *The Narcissus Theme in Western European Literature up to the Early Nineteenth Century.* Lund: Gleerups, 1967.

Warner, Eric. *The Waves.* Cambridge: Cambridge University Press, 1987.

White, J. J. "Signs of Disturbance: The Semiological Import of Some Recent Fiction by Michel Tournier and Peter Handke." *Journal of European Studies* 4 (1974): 223–54.

Whitmont, Edward C. *The Symbolic Quest.* Princeton, N.J.: Princeton University Press, 1978.

Wilden, Anthony. "Lacan and the Discourse of the Other." In *Speech and Language in Psychoanalysis.* Baltimore: Johns Hopkins University Press, 1968.

Woodcock, Bruce. "Escaping the Script: The Politics of Change." *Male Mythologies: John Fowles and Masculinity.* Totowa, N.J.: Barnes & Noble, 1984.

Woolf, Virginia. *The Waves.* In *Jacob's Room and The Waves: Two Complete Novels.* New York: Harcourt, Brace & World, 1959.

——. *A Writer's Diary.* Ed. Leonard Woolf. New York: Harcourt, Brace & World, 1953.

Wright, Elizabeth. *Psychoanalytic Criticism: Theory in Practice.* London: Methuen, 1984.

Yeats, W. B. *The Collected Poems.* New York: Macmillan, 1974.

Index